THE RAPTURE INDEX

A SUBURBAN BESTIARY

MOLLY REID

THE RAPTURE INDEX

A SUBURBAN BESTIARY

AMERICAN READER SERIES, NO. 32

BOA EDITIONS, LTD. ❖ ROCHESTER, NY ❖ 2019

First Edition
19 20 21 22 7 6 5 4 3 2 1

For information about permission to reuse any material from this book, please contact The Permissions Company at www.permissionscompany.com or e-mail permdude@gmail.com.

Publications by BOA Editions, Ltd.—a not-for-profit corporation under section 501 (c) (3) of the United States Internal Revenue Code—are made possible with funds from a variety of sources, including public funds from the Literature Program of the National Endowment for the Arts; the New York State Council on the Arts, a state agency; and the County of Monroe, NY. Private funding sources include the Max and Marian Farash Charitable Foundation; the Mary S. Mulligan Charitable Trust; the Rochester Area Community Foundation; the Ames-Amzalak Memorial Trust in memory of Henry Ames, Semon Amzalak, and Dan Amzalak; and contributions from many individuals nationwide. See Colophon on page 222 for special individual acknowledgments.

Cover Art: "Claws" by Elizabeth Albert
Cover Design: Sandy Knight
Interior Design and Composition: Richard Foerster
BOA Logo: Mirko

Library of Congress Cataloging-in-Publication Data

Names: Reid, Molly (Molly Jean), author.
Title: The rapture index : a suburban bestiary / Molly Reid.
Description: First edition. | Rochester, NY : BOA Edtions, Ltd., [2019] |
  Series: American reader series ; no. 32 | Includes index.
Identifiers: LCCN 2018050145 (print) | LCCN 2018055220 (ebook) | ISBN
  9781942683810 (ebook) | ISBN 9781942683803 (paperback : alk. paper)
Subjects: LCSH: Human-animal relationships—Fiction. | Suburbs—Fiction.
Classification: LCC PS3618.E543 (ebook) | LCC PS3618.E543 R37 2019 (print) |

  DDC 813/.6—dc23
LC record available at https://lccn.loc.gov/2018050145

BOA Editions, Ltd.
250 North Goodman Street, Suite 306
Rochester, NY 14607
www.boaeditions.org
A. Poulin, Jr., Founder (1938–1996)

Contents

Happy You're Here

This hospital is across the street from a beach on which the body of a blue whale has washed ashore. Each time I visit the whale, I am not alone. People line the bluff, put down blankets by the rocks. The brave ones get close. They come from the town and also outside the town, bloated-whale-carcass tourists.

A laminated piece of paper taped to a light pole provides basic facts and a photograph: long and sleek, fins like carved wax, swimming in watery blue light. Average life span: 80 to 90 years. Size: 80 to 105 feet. Weight: up to 200 tons. Did you know? The tongue of a blue whale can weigh as much as an elephant.

This one lolling in the waste of the tideline doesn't look like the picture. Dark strips peel from its gray-brown body like rubber paint, barnacles jagged and melting. The carcass is swollen with methane gas, is swelling even now, as I stand at the hospital window. The town is probably worried it will explode—nobody knows what havoc that much flying blubber could wreak.

·:·

I think about the time our mother was convinced she had Lou Gehrig's disease because she was having difficulty swallowing. It turned out to be some kind of allergy, but in the year before she went to the doctor she conducted elaborate healing rituals and gave long-winded speeches preparing us for her death. A shaman, a white-haired woman in a pink knit sweater, skull tattoo on her forearm withered to an acorn, came over to lead and expedite the process. At twelve years old, I learned about the four domains of vibration and light. That during the journey into death, we engage with the soul level, the domain of myth. This domain was always where my mother felt most comfortable.

I try to remember what we did during that year, the actual rituals, but all I can conjure is the smell of sage burning, the drip of blessed castor oil down my mother's arms.

⁘

The spotted hawk swoops by, my brother intones, *and accuses me, he complains of my gab and my loitering.*

I point out a sliver of ocean from the window like a tourist. Her eyes are closed. It's hard to tell if she's sleeping or listening, her face blank as the moon.

It started with fever and disorientation. Her white blood count is high. Elevated AST and ALT the doctor says, though he does not say what this means and we do not ask. Why don't we ask? We nod, mimic his intellectual puzzlement and detached concern. We've eliminated leukemia and myelofibrosis, he says. His *we* clearly distinct from ours, though maybe this is reassuring.

We've also ruled out the hepatitises, other unpronounceable ailments—diseases of blood, bones, glands. Her body is a map washed clean. Or with too many towns and rivers, a muck of dots and squiggles rendering the names of things incomprehensible.

Though I don't really get it—I don't remember our mother ever reading *Song of Myself,* or any Walt Whitman, she was more an Emily Dickinson/Rumi fan—I don't want my brother to stop. I don't want to take our mother's hand in silence, her skin dry and unresponsive and so pliant touch seems dangerous. *I sound my barbaric yawp over the roofs of the world.*

"I think she likes it," Daniel says, holding up the book.
"How can you tell?"

He looks at her and doesn't answer me.

⁘

My mother wrote novels under a pseudonym, her books
popular with a very specific readership. Picture bare feet and
crystals, Chinese herbs and incense. Characters with names
like Starwarrior and Moonriot. Except she hasn't written
anything in ten years, since she moved to this seaside town
to live the rest of her days in obscurity.

This hospital room is like any hospital room. Beige lam-
inate floors. Stiff rubber curtains. Beeping screens and bags
of fluid with tubes snaking in and out of my mother. Plastic
handles on the bed to hold onto, or to strap down a body.

⁘

Your birth, my mother used to say, wistfully and with-
out irony, *was the first time I experienced real loss.*

I was born at gunpoint, above a bar in an apartment
with a leaky roof and a view of the bank across the street.
The bar was named after a president or general, something
with heft, dignity, though my mother could never remem-
ber it. What she did remember was the noise of other peo-
ple having fun, a roar and shush like the ocean, punctured
by breaking glass. Smells through the vents that made her
mouth water, cravings she could never satiate no matter
how many syrup and mayonnaise sandwiches, maraschino
cherries in gravy.

She was in the shower when she heard noises that she
thought were my father home for his lunch break. At this
point in the story she usually adds that he had a broken
arm—a drunken fall down the stairs connecting bar and
apartment—and in addition to being nine months pregnant,

she had to navigate his self-pity and wash his hair in the sink every day before work. (Thin black hairs curled against wet porcelain. Shampoo in his eye. Pressing her swollen breasts against his teeth to shut him up.)

She heard thuds and clinking over the water, like someone looking for something, someone in a rush, like my father had misplaced his wallet again. But when she got out of the shower, there was instead a stranger in their bedroom.

The man pointed a gun at my naked mother and asked her to give him all her money. When she told him she didn't have any, he looked worried, glancing at the half moon of her belly and then out the window. The man was young with golden hair and thick lashes, a scar that ran from hairline to chin. There was something about this man that made the hairs on the back of my mother's neck stand on end, something beyond the gun in his hands. His scar was a deep crease that marked half his face from the other, as if someone had ripped it in two then put it back together a little off, not lining up the edges quite, so that everything on the right side was a little lower than the left. But the hairs on the back of my mother's neck did not rise because she was afraid or disgusted. She recognized him from her dreams.

In the middle of a swimming pool in the backyard of a house on a cul-de-sac; glossy-leaved ashes lining bright wide sidewalks; the water pleasantly warm and turquoise; bodies floating all around her and a current that tries to pull her under. Then this man with a scar pulls her up up up, until she's flying above it all.

The robber was the man from her dream. He seemed to recognize it too, at the same moment she did, but neither of them knew what to do with the information. So they stood like that—my mother with her breasts bared, hand on the globe of stretched skin where inside a child, I, was furiously churning, the man holding the gun with both hands like a rope that would pull him home—for one long elastic minute.

Finally, my mother said to the man, "Turn around." He lowered his gun, faced the wall while she put on some clothes. With his back turned, he took everything out of his bulging pockets: some of her jewelry, car keys, a small hand-painted Kali statue she'd picked up on a college trip to Delhi, other things that weren't hers too: a long peacock feather, an antique gold watch, sunflower seeds, the skin of a rattlesnake that he handled with extraordinary care—set it all on the bed, and left without looking back.

My mother's water broke then, and the owner of the bar took her kicking and screaming to the hospital.

Even my own birth, I am not the center of the story.

Daniel has left. I didn't bring anything to read, so I tell her about the whale across the street, about the tourists flocking, line of cars parked along the road. There is someone, an official, keeping everyone back.

She gives zero indication of interest. Though her eyes are open, they look beyond me, somewhere I can't see. Her characteristic dreads are gone, her hair now thin and see-through as the fog. I don't know what it is she wants, but she clearly wants something. I know this feeling, this look.

I've tried my whole life to not be my mother. I make many lists. I never run out of gas. I refill my prescriptions early. I have never waited until they turn the lights off to pay my electric bill. Have never left my daughter to wait for me all afternoon outside school because I forgot what time it was, because I got carried away with a poem or a record or the light on the river, a pattern so synchronous and dazzling it swallowed whole hours.

I was always too boring. Uninterested in dyeing my dolls' hair wild colors or cutting magazine pages into snowflakes or pretending to be a creature that doesn't exist.

I would catch her looking at me sometimes as if at a stranger on the subway. Sizing me up. Guessing at what I kept in my pockets.

The nurse comes in and adjusts things, writes something down on her clipboard.

"She's happy you're here," she says, even though my mother's expression has not changed since I arrived.

I go on about the whale, how sad it is really; it probably stranded because of the sonar. I've read about this: the Navy's practice explosions disrupt the whales' feeding and diving patterns, their ability to communicate. I wonder if it came on shore alive, if people failed to notice. All around a spectacle of human failure.

Eventually my mother interrupts my babbling. "I remember you," she says. "Come here. You smell so good." The tubes in her nose—how can she smell anything? "Powdered sugar," she says. "Donuts." I lean in and try to give her a hug, the bones in her arms small and delicate as a cat's.

At sunset I walk down the street again to the whale. A larger crowd than earlier, children held back by worried mothers, couples huddled together in the cold. Khaki shirts mill around the carcass. Some of them have clipboards. Others seem to be investigating a large machine. They gesture and pace.

If it's possible, the whale has gotten even bigger. Its surface sways and ripples in the wind. The stink is strong; some people hold their arm or the flap of their jacket over their nose and mouth.

"What are they doing?" I ask a woman holding a small child.

"They're going to blow it up," she says. The child twists in her arms, straining to get a better look.

"How are they going to do that?"

The woman shrugs. "They brought in some kind of explosives expert."

"Is it safe to be out here?"

"They told us to stay up on the bluff. But they said they can't be sure what will happen."

More people arrive. Blankets are set down, picnic baskets opened. Cheap champagne poured into plastic cups. This is something. An event. A man on the beach stalks the whale with a tape measure. He must be the expert.

We stand for a long while and watch nothing happen. People begin to get antsy. Games are started on the blankets, *tic-tic-tic* of cards laid down. Guitars are strummed, an off-key sing-along to Michael Jackson's "Will You Be There" that peters out in the middle. Finally, after extensive discussion between the expert and other people in khaki suits, the explosion event is called off. A man in a nice blue button-down shirt comes by to tell everyone.

"Sorry, folks," he says. "We've received word from above it's too dangerous."

"From God?" someone asks.

"What are you going to do with the whale?" A little boy, the same one from earlier, asks.

"We don't know yet, buddy."

"Are you going to push him back into the sea?" he asks. "Maybe."

The man moves down the line, and the little boy calls after him, "What if he explodes right now?" But the man acts like he doesn't hear him.

People begin packing up, folding their blankets and putting lids on Tupperware containers.

"What do we do?" The little boy asks his mother, and I turn to her, too, as if we're a unit.

"We go home, I guess," she says.

When my mother first moved here, she bought a small motorboat. She'd never been in a boat before in her life, let alone driven one, didn't know a thing about navigation or docking or currents (she obviously did not take the legal route of permits and licenses.) The first time she took it on the ocean, she got lost. Went out and out, until she ran out of fuel, and then she drifted, not another boat in sight for hours. Nightfall came, and she still hadn't seen even a speck on the horizon.

A fisherman saved her. (Wild gray beard and big rubber boots. Scar from hairline to jaw—of course it was the man from her dreams, the one who'd tried to rob her thirty years earlier, having traded a life of crime for the sea.) The sun went down, water rippled fire. With his pocketknife the fisherman shucked oysters and tipped the pale salty meat to her lips. They shared stories and clear rum, and by the time they got to the shore, they were in love. This is the story (summarized here) we received in the mail. The envelope was addressed to both of us, though it arrived at Daniel's and he had to read it to me over the phone.

Shortly after this, my mother refused any visits. She stopped taking our phone calls. When I showed up on her doorstep, I had to coax her into letting me inside.

We sat together on the couch in her living room while she calmly said insane things. The fisherman was there. Or someone who could have been the fisherman; he was not introduced to me. This man didn't have a scar, but he did have a beard that looked like it had weathered some storms. He sat whittling at the kitchen counter. Nodded to me as I came in, gave my mother a look that was like, *Do you want me to take care of this?*

My mother said she was starting over. She had something inside her, a ball or stone, something bad, rotten, and she was going to live here by the ocean with the fisherman while it got bigger. That's what she called him, *the fisherman*.

"What, do you mean like a tumor? Have you been to the doctor?" I asked.

She said no, not like a tumor, more metaphysical than that, like a wish or a grudge or a ghost living in her heart.

"Is it that you miss Dad? We all miss him."

But she said no, it wasn't like that either. She leaned over and dipped her fingers into my glass of water as if testing its temperature, then flicked the water in my general direction like a blessing. Thin curls of wood fell like snow around the fisherman's feet.

She had to cut all ties, a psychic had told her. In order to purify the body of memory and the expectations of others.

What about the fisherman?

"He has none."

I told her that not everything is a story. Life doesn't give you symbols.

She looked out the window at her lemon tree and smiled.

Before I left, the fisherman unfurled what he'd been whittling: a long chain, each link meticulously sculpted and smoothed. It was at least ten feet long. He began to wrap it around my mother, starting at her neck, winding down her shoulders, her arms.

"You shouldn't be here for this," she said.

Where is her fisherman now?

"They don't know who that is," Daniel says. "Nobody

has come but us."

⋮

"A young woman walks down a hallway following a man in a white coat," my mother would start, her voice low and conspiratorial. "She doesn't know why. There's something about him. He seems to know where he's going. He disappears behind a door. She waits just outside and hears voices, familiar voices. And something else, a sickening familiar hum like the curdle of milk"—this was how she talked, exactly how she wrote, *hum like the curdle of milk*, and her eyes would widen a little, having pleased herself—"She turns the knob and opens the door."

Frozen in the headlights of her expectancy. A look of such hope, as if there was a real possibility I could be her creative partner.

"What's behind the door?" she'd prod.

"A couch?"

"Okay. What else? Is the man there? What is he doing?"

"Sitting on the couch?"

⋮

There is a different nurse in the room when I return, changing the bag of my mother's drip. He acknowledges me with a nod. I'm starting to understand the rotation and the ways the energy shifts. This one I think of as the efficient one, all business.

"How is she doing?" I ask him.

"She's comfortable. Her heart sped up a little earlier, but we gave her something."

"What does that mean?"

The nurse shrugs. "It happens."

He moves around my mother's body and makes small adjustments, repositions pillows and gently lifts up each shoulder, hip, leg.

"Have you been to see the whale?" I ask, trying to look anywhere but the loose skin around my mother's elbow.

"What whale?"

"The one across the street? The reason all the people are here?"

He gives me an odd look, pulls the blanket up to my mother's chin.

"Has the doctor come by?" I try instead.

"A few hours ago."

"Can I talk to him?"

"He'll be back in the morning."

"What if something happens before then?"

He takes a folder from the door and writes something down, then turns. "She's happy you're here," he says.

Daniel was seven, and I was eight. There was a park around the corner from our house where we were allowed to go by ourselves, as long as we were together. Designed to resemble a thoroughfare: a loop of sidewalk that went up and down hills and into tunnels and around to a fake filling station. Big yellow speed bumps we would pry from the sidewalk and carry home like medals.

On this day, once we started going around on our bikes, we noticed a man sitting on one of the benches off the loop. He was wearing a big brown rumpled coat though it was a sunny summer day. Every time I passed him, he smiled and gave a little wave, and I wondered if I was supposed to know him. Maybe he was a parent, or a teacher, or one of our mother's weird friends. So I smiled back, showing off a little, catching air where the concrete bucked, going fast around the corners. Daniel ignored him, and I tried to make up for this act of rudeness. I was always having to be the gracious one.

"Hey," the man eventually said after my fourth loop. I stopped my bike and let Daniel pass me.

"You're really fast," the man said. One of his arms was missing. The left one was there like normal, the hand emerging from the cuff of his coat. But on the right side, the fabric hung deflated from his shoulder.

"Thanks," I said. I could tell then that something was wrong. I realized I didn't know this man. The way he was looking at me was not right. He was too nervous. Too excited. His whole body trembled.

"What's your name?" he asked.

"Bea," I said.

"What?" he asked. "Why don't you come over here for a minute—you're so far away, I can't hear you."

When I got closer, I realized he did have a right arm, and that it was doing something under his coat. I looked around, but Daniel was no longer in the park. Nobody was. It was just this man and me. Feeling embarrassed. Knowing I should run, but not how. The man opened his coat then. His penis, pink and distended, curved out of a patch of wiry black hair like a fungus. The tip of it bulged from the top of his grip, the skin worked by his hand crinkling like tissue paper. With his other hand he reached out to me, and only then did I run.

I ran past my bike as fast as I could out of the park and around the corner to our house. When I came through the door, Daniel was in the kitchen with our mother, who was tying up sprigs of lavender. Clumps of purple flowers dangled upside down from string that looped from one side of the kitchen to the other. The lavender would stay that way for weeks, and I still now associate this memory with its smell, a sharp herbal scent that seems to find me everywhere.

As soon as I saw her, I began to cry.

"Why didn't you come back with your brother?" she demanded. Daniel looked away, having obviously told her something to exonerate himself. "Where is your bike?"

I tried to tell her about the man and what I saw, but I couldn't find the right words. I kept looking to Daniel, but he didn't meet my eyes. I was shaking.

"Come on," she said. "Both of you, let's go." She clipped the sprig in her hand to the string and marched out the front door. I trailed her, feeling vindicated and scared, not knowing what would happen when she saw the man in the overcoat, but knowing that something would.

Except he was gone. There was a very young boy being pushed by his mother on a three-wheeler, and my bike was still lying where I'd left it on the path, but the bench was empty.

My mother turned to me. "Where is he?"

"I don't know," I said. I pointed. "He was right there."

"Did he disappear?"

I shook my head.

"Get your bike," she said. Daniel ran ahead and I pushed my bike behind her, feeling the tears well and then turn into something else in my throat.

Before we went into the house, she stopped. "You can't make up stories like that," she said. She leaned in close, her dreads fraying ropes that tickled the tops of my shoulders. Patchouli and lavender. I tried to say I know, I tried to say that's not what I was doing at all, but the words stuck.

She crouched down beside me and put her hands on my hips.

"You walked over to the man in the brown coat," she said gently. "The man called you over and so you went." I nodded. "He wanted to show you something." I nodded.

"He reached into his pocket. What was in his pocket? What did he pull out?"

Daniel whacked the bushes with a trowel from the flowerbed. *Take that*, he said, *and that.*

"A gold coin," I said. She smiled and squeezed my hips. *You're going to pay*, Daniel said to the bush.

"It was beautiful," I said. She waited. "It had the face of a woman, a beautiful woman, the queen of a faraway place."

"A magic coin," my mother said. I nodded. A magic coin.

A squirrel ran from Daniel's exhortations and scrambled up the oak tree in our front yard. My mother pulled a long sprig of lavender from the pocket of her dress and tucked the end of it behind my ear.

On the way to the beach, I pass shops advertising clam chowder, saltwater taffy, glass beads and watercolor seascapes. Most of them are closed, because it's Sunday, or because it's the winter season, or just because people make their own hours around here. The ocean on the other side of the shops roars with the freeway.

Her organs are shutting down. They've put her on dialysis, they're giving her morphine. Tomorrow she'll be moved to hospice.

What about the antibiotics? What about the liver transplant?

"I'm sorry," the doctor said. "She's not responding. She doesn't qualify."

But that's what she does, I didn't say, that's her thing— She hates tests! You have to tell it to her god-brain!

I nodded, I signed something.

Daniel has left for good. Or at least, until the funeral— though this is something that is not said. Only implied, with his apologies and his relief. He has a family to get back to, a wife and two sons.

"Besides," he said in a rare moment of candor, "she doesn't have any idea what's happening."

There are only a few people along the bluff now, mostly couples on blankets clutching each other like children.

A mutilation is underway. People gather around the carcass with hacksaws and buckets. Some of the people saw back and forth. Others stand with their entire arms inside the whale. Blood, intestines and other unidentifiable organs splay on the sand. I can't look at it. I can't look away. The fog has lifted, clouds stitched together with molten orange thread, which lends the whole scene a grisly apocalyptic quality.

A woman beside me throws up in a patch of scrub brush.

"Are you okay?" I ask her.

She folds her arms over her chest, bends slightly at the waist. She's pale, and there's still a bit of something in the corner of her mouth.

"I'm fine," she says. "I think I ate something bad."

I recognize her. She's one of my mother's nurses. The nice one. Young and pretty, big brown eyes.

"This is awful," I say, gesturing to the whale.

"I know," she says. "I'm afraid it's only going to get worse."

We stand together with our hands in our pockets, looking everywhere but at the whale. The sun dips down to the ocean and the whole thing lights up golden for a moment, and then the muted blue of twilight sets in. Most everyone has left except the nurse and me. But she seems preoccupied by another matter. She stares out at the ocean, every once in a while moving her lips as if in prayer.

A dog rushes up to us then, a big slobbering speckled mutt. I squat down to pet him, and he drops a dark wet something at my feet: seaweed or blubber, I'm not asking questions. As I chuck the something down the sand, I try to say a little prayer, too.

Back at the hospital, the fisherman is there. He stands inside the doorway, a hulking tower of a man, smelling like the sea and carrying the fog in his beard. Neither half of his face betrays any emotion. A bright orange bucket at his feet. He is staring at my mother when I come in, and she at him, and I have to wonder what kind of communication I have interrupted.

He turns to me and nods.

"Hungry?" he asks.

I am. He gets to work. He spreads newspaper carefully over my mother like a blanket, slices a lemon into slender wedges on the tray beside her bed. Removes a knobby white horseradish root from his pocket and grates it onto the newspaper.

He gestures for me to sit beside her, then lugs the bucket over and begins to shuck the oysters one by one. I squeeze the lemon, dab the horseradish. Slide the meat into my mouth, savoring the initial resistance between my teeth, then the soft gush. Eyes closed, I try to tease out nuance: seaweed, melon, smoke. The crunch of silt. He sucks them down with me on the other side of her hospital bed. We place the shells on the newspaper, on her body. She watches us.

In one of the oysters, I find a pearl. I remove it from my mouth and hold it up to the light. The fisherman grunts and hands me the next half shell.

"Legend says they are tears of the gods," he says.

"They're good luck," my mother says, her voice strange and scratchy.

The fisherman tips a shell to her lips and she takes the oyster into her mouth, closes her eyes to swallow. I'm not sure if this is something she should have, but I'm not willing to take it away from her either.

We finish the rest of the oysters quietly, and then the fisherman rolls up the newspaper and takes his bucket and leaves. Barely a trace of him after that, the faintest whiff of seawater. A peacock feather laid at her side.

I place the pearl in my mother's palm, tell her, again, about the whale.

It was beautiful, I whisper into her ear. *Flying blubber like falling stars, seagulls swooping and screeching, the whole beach in flames.*

BESTIARY I: The Neighbor's Bees

The neighbor's bees are harmless. Their behavior is nearly identical to wild honeybees. One queen for each colony. Workers clean cells, feed larvae, collect pollen, guard the entrance. Drones have a singular duty: mate with new queens and fertilize them during mating flights sometimes several hundred feet in the air. When their duty is over, the bees in colder climates will drive the drones out of the hive to die, biting and tearing at their legs and wings. There is, after all, only so much nectar to go around.

Most amateur beekeepers are careful not to overextend their resources or take on more bees than they can manage. You may hear buzzing, especially in the summer months, and one or two could venture into your yard, expert pollen-carriers for lemon trees and azaleas.

The neighbor's bees are typical in every way but one: These bees seem to be highly attuned to human passion, can sense when the desire centers of the brain have switched on. They've been reported to swarm the lustful. Teenagers making out behind the school. Newlyweds fooling around in the privacy of their own backyard. Mr. Griffin from city council who was, he claimed, simply walking past Elizabeth McKenzie's house one Saturday night.

Some say it started with Harriet on Snowapple. On her first vision quest, a bee accompanied her into the light, and now she thinks she has an affinity, a spiritual contract. Every fifth Wednesday, she smears herself with the pheromones of fifty queens and dances around her cul-de-sac, a thick buzzing fur from the waist up.

They started out her bees, but I think they've mixed with other bees in the neighborhood, and it's confusing now. Many have chosen to cool it on the public displays of affection. But I say the opposite. I say use it to your advantage.

Maybe you find yourself with the kettle about to boil for some tea. Out of honey, you knock on the neighbor's door, and he answers in his white beekeeping suit—a dreamy Buddhist astronaut. Follow him inside. Make him follow you outside. Unzip the mesh veil. Sink your teeth where the elastic has left a notched halo around his ankle. If the bees begin to gather, don't panic. Let the stings remind you of the places on your body you've forgotten. Confess to him your heart has always seemed to need a box. You understand the logic of hexagons, smoke sleep, turning dust into sugar. If his wife comes home and starts to shout or engage in physically aggressive behavior, step aside. Let her carry him off. If she needs help, offer to take a leg.

The Permutations of A

There is something Beatrice is doing in the kitchen, but it's anybody's guess. She has both hands on the counter, head turned to the side and tilted, thick black hair sprouting from a high ponytail like an illustration of a girl with a ponytail. Beatrice often finds herself lost in thought in this exact location. She doesn't consciously go but is pulled as if in a dream, and then, once she assumes the position, her mind begins its agitations. Like now. She is solving. Analyzing all possible outcomes. Working out, with mathematical precision, all the permutations of A, the profusion of ways that A can lead to B, transmogrify into Z, or grow wings, fuzz open and become a hexagon filled with wax and honey.

A is Alice, Beatrice's daughter. She is down the hall in the bathroom, where she has been for the last hour putting on makeup. Not the kind typically expected of a sixteen-year-old girl. The stuff used in zombie movies and gore fests: high-end Halloween shit. Today she is perfecting gouged-out eyeballs. Which is difficult because to get the full effect you have to close your eyes, so she has to keep taking close-eyed selfies in the mirror and then trying to correct the mistakes she sees on the small screen. She uses liquid latex, tissues, food coloring, wax, two different shades of lip liner, and cornstarch. She is almost done. Almost to that sweet spot where she doesn't recognize herself in the mirror.

Beatrice is a medical illustrator. She specializes in forensic reconstruction, hired by hospitals and lawyers to reconstruct the details of contested surgeries. Illustrate the various ways a body failed, how science and human error failed a body. A slipped stitch, organs stapled to other organs, sponges left in abdomens. One would think this line of work would situate her to embrace her daughter's new hobby. But perhaps it is one thing to create a computer graphic of what was supposed to be a routine appendectomy that due to the operating surgeon's inexperience led instead to the removal of an ovary. Quite another to round the corner and see your sixteen-year-old daughter with a rusty nail sticking out of her cheek, puss and blood bubbling down her chin.

"You can't go to school like that."

"Why not?"

"Because you look like you've been dead for a long while and a huge chunk of your cheek is missing."

Alice beams. "Other girls wear makeup to school."

"Take it off."

"But it takes forever. I'll be late. See this? It's wax. Do you know how hard that is to get off?"

"Fine. But if anybody asks, you did this without my permission."

Alice's father expired from the rupture of a cerebral aneurysm six months ago. So sudden there was nothing anyone could do. They were standing in the kitchen when he turned to Beatrice with a strange look, panic and something maybe like smug regret, said his head hurt and then put his hands to his face and cried out. She dialed 911, but he died before they arrived, crumpled to the floor almost gracefully, like a dog exhausted after a long walk. This is not the reason Alice puts on her makeup. It isn't as simple as that. There is the body, and then there is the soul, and she likes to separate them.

At school, Alice walks through the hallways like a movie star. Kids snap pictures of her. They part. Point her out. Never has she been so popular.

In social studies third period, Mark Jacobson asks to borrow a pencil then says he likes her puss. How did she get the bubble like that?

"A secret."

"Wanna meet after school underneath the bleachers?"

"Zombies don't date."

"I wasn't talking about dating," he says. His eyes are clear and bright vampire blue.

Beatrice is working on the dimensions of a perforated small intestine when the doorbell rings. There is a young man on her doorstep who would like to speak with her about the grace of God. She invites him in, offers him tea, then realizes she doesn't have any so heats up some old coffee in the microwave. The boy seems surprised at being invited in, and a little unprepared. He riffles through his pamphlets.

"So what do I have to do?" Beatrice asks.

"What do you mean?" the boy says.

"To have grace. To get in God's good graces."

"Grace is divine help and strength that we receive through the atonement of Jesus Christ," the boy recites. "Through grace, we are saved from sin and death."

"But what exactly is it—grace?"

"Grace is an enabling power that strengthens us from day to day and helps us endure to the end."

"But if you were going to liken it to something?" she asks.

"Umm," the boy says.

"I need a good metaphor."

He thinks, opens one of his pamphlets, looks out the window. "I don't know," he says. "Pancakes?"

She tries to think of something, anything, to keep him here.

"Do you want to pray?" she asks. "Are you hungry? Do you want a cookie?"

He looks around, gazes longingly at the front door. "Is your husband home?"

Underneath the bleachers empty beer cans, cigarette butts, fast-food wrappers, a glut of neon plastic straws and, inexplicably, an enormous tuft of white fur stuck to the grass: an animal without a body. Mark Jacobson is kissing the side of Alice's neck. It's a little too wet for her tastes, but the sensation overall is pleasant. Their mouths kiss for a while, and then he pulls away, breathing heavily.

"Wanna go to the Scoresby house on Saturday?" he says. "Some people going. You know, because haunted." He is having some trouble making complete sentences, something that maybe he always had trouble with but she never noticed until now because he had only ever asked her to borrow a pencil. "Having a séance. And beer."

Out of the corner of her eye, Alice sees the tuft move, as if perking up its ears. Mark Jacobson runs his lips over the gash on her forehead, over the bumpy part, and it is like she both feels and doesn't feel it, the gash a part of her and not a part of her, and every part of her responds.

The boy has accepted a cookie. Beatrice doesn't have the heart to tell him it's an edible. She's been having trouble sleeping, and pot is the only thing that seems to help, except she doesn't like smoking it. So cookies. Sometimes brownies. She gets them from a shop just over the state line in Washington. Worried that Alice might get into them, she hides the paper bag in the back of the pantry, behind stacks of untouched soup cans.

She's not entirely sure why she must keep the boy here. Maybe she wants answers from God, though she has never believed in the capital-G. Her faith resides more in something like a string of energy holding the world together, a spiritual seam with which everything trembles in harmony. But maybe this is because she'd never gotten to know capital-G. Maybe this boy and his literature can provide insight into why her daughter barely speaks to her anymore, why she'd rather hole up in the bathroom painting herself a murder victim. She usually only has half a cookie, but she gives the boy a whole one.

Alice has to pass an interview in order to participate in the séance. A girl named Valerie approaches her at school the next day, leads her to the back of the science building where the cool kids smoke cigarettes, and asks her a series of questions. Do you believe in ghosts? And, Are you afraid of ghosts? And, Have you lost someone you wish to contact? Valerie has long black hair with heavy bangs cut in a pencil-straight line above her thick black eyebrows and she wears black eyeliner drawn out from the corners of her eyelids like cat eyes and Alice is impressed with her no-nonsense attitude. Alice answers yes, no, and yes. Valerie confirms her acceptance into the group, with the stipulation that she could be dismissed if she in any way disrupted the energy in the room or failed to fully believe.

"Oh," she adds, "and don't do the makeup thing. It will confuse them."

Alice wants to object. After all, if Valerie could wear her goth goop, why couldn't Alice express herself as suited her disposition? But she decides to keep her mouth shut on this one. Valerie tells Alice to come on Saturday night with at least two prepared questions.

"We might not get to all of them," Valerie says, "but above all else, a séance must have structure."

Before Alice was born, Alice's father and Beatrice were like halves of the same body. One would reach for the other, the other's arm already outstretched. They'd fall asleep after making love, limbs entangled, sweat commingling, his hand in her hair, her shoulder cupped in his armpit, then wake hungry and throbbing and slide into each other like eels. They didn't talk much but when they did, their words made love too. She was convinced they communicated telepathically. She only had to think banana, and he would peel it for her. But after Alice was born, a tectonic shift occurred. The love she felt for her daughter was blinding, conflagrant. It consumed her completely. She thought at first it was hormones, would stop once she stopped breastfeeding. But she grew more and more indifferent to her husband's advances, to his declarations and pleadings. And then eventually, he seemed to give up, too. He worked longer hours. Developed a running habit. Their exchanges became affable and good-natured, like coworkers who respect each other but don't hang out on the weekends, their old telepathy now rooted in domestic routine. She always thought the fire would come back, that they had time to bring it back. In the moment before he put his head in his hands and crumpled to the floor, Alice's father, in slightly slurred speech, said, "Why are you just standing there?"

"Using candles helps to create a spiritual atmosphere," Valerie says. There is a Ouija board and a glass of water on the table. Mark Jacobson already groped her a little in the car, but Alice is way less interested in him now than in the dark candlelit room, in Valerie's serious eyebrows, in the way the floorboards creak under her feet like someone's dying breath.

There are few preliminaries. Basic introductions are made, and then they—there are five of them: Alice, Mark Jacobson, Valerie, a chubby boy with a septum piercing and green hair introduced as Shrek, and another boy who looks like James Dean with a Mohawk—are seated around the table holding hands. Alice hides an oozing sore on the side of her neck with her hair; she mostly obeyed Valerie's request but needed something to calm her down, to ground her. It itches—she may have used too much liquid latex—but without her hands it's difficult to get at. Lifting her shoulder to her ear brings some relief. Alice holds Mark Jacobson's clammy hand with her right and James Dean's with her left. James Dean's hand is soft, cool, and dry, like one of the smooth round stones she liked to gather near the river, rubbing her thumb over them in her pocket on the walk home. They are silent a long while, eyes closed, nothing but the sound of their breath. Alice feels herself relaxing. The energy in the room unfolds, opens. For a moment she is light and outside herself, like deep kissing or floating in the ocean. Then Valerie speaks.

"I'm sorry, Mark Jacobson, but I'm going to have to ask you to leave."

Mark Jacobson is incredulous.

"You are disrupting the energy in the room," Valerie says. "Your mind is elsewhere. We need complete surrender."

"Okay," he says. "Am sorry. Try harder."

"No," Valerie says. "Goodbye."

He looks at Alice, but she looks away.

The boy is staring at his hand. He slowly opens and closes his fingers, then turns it over and inspects his palm.

"Can you imagine," he says, his words moving as if through water, "a nail straight through your palm."

Beatrice looks at her own hand. She'd only had two bites of a cookie but can already feel it, her skin carbonating, thoughts drifting, a pleasant paranoia that keeps her alert and vivid.

"Hey," he says, looking suddenly up at her, the spark of an idea glinting in his heavy-lidded eyes.

"What?"

"I like you," he says.

She is probably more pleased than she should be. "Thank you," she says.

"People are usually too busy. They don't answer the door, even though I can see they're home. I can hear them talking. Their kids laughing. Or they're smug you know, say they know all about God's grace. As if I can't possibly know about it like they do. Or sometimes they insult me."

"People are terrible."

"Yes." His expression becomes very serious. Then, just as quickly, he breaks into a goofy grin. "What was in that cookie?"

She smiles. She wonders what Alice would say if she were to come home, if she were to walk in and see her, someone who opens her front door, who provides shelter and sustenance.

"That's a really cool painting," he says, pointing to the far wall.

"Oh, thanks," she says. "I painted that in college." She tilts her head. It was one of her more experimental pieces, an elephant with a pig nose in a birthday hat, looking disgruntled and surrounded by small, happy rodents dancing and carousing and drinking champagne. Alice's father hated that painting, and she only hung it after he died.

"Do you still paint?" he asks.

She shakes her head. "Mostly I do computer graphics. Sometimes I draw, if I get stuck."

"Ooh," the boy grunts. "Let's draw something!"

She shrugs and fetches some drawing paper and charcoal pencils.

"What should we draw?" she asks, smoothing the paper on the coffee table.

The boy closes his eyes and takes a deep breath, opens his left eye.

"God," he says.

The first questions are yes or no. The four of them each have a finger on the planchette. Valerie acts as medium. First Valerie asks, Is there a spirit here? which moves the planchette to YES, though it feels forced and very slow, like one of them, or all of them, are moving it with a slight pressure, a little bit at a time.

Then Valerie asks, "Are you happy?"

The planchette moves, again a little uninspired, to NO.

After this, Valerie is silent for a moment. A breeze moves through the room. Valerie asks, "How did you die?"

And this time the planchette moves with force, quickly, from letter to letter: M-U-R-D-E-R. Alice shivers. It has dropped ten degrees in the last ten seconds. The water in the glass trembles.

"What is your name?"

No answer.

"What would you like to tell us?" This is Alice's question.

She holds her finger as light as she can without taking it off the planchette.

Y-O-U-R-M-O-T-H-E-R.

It stops.

"Your mother," Valerie says. "Whose mother?"

No movement.

"Your mother what?"

There is a pause, and then, D-I-D-N-O-T-H-I-N-G.

"Did not hing?" Shrek asks, and is shushed.

"Did nothing," Valerie says. "Did nothing when?" she asks.

No movement.

"Okay," she says after another pause, "Do you know Alice's father?" This is Alice's second question.

Y-O-U-C-O-U-L-D-S-A-Y-T-H-A-T.

"Are you Alice's father?" Valerie asks, and Alice looks at her. Valerie looks strange, her eyes unfocused, a flush in her cheeks. "What would you like to say to Alice?" she asks. This is clearly off-script. The planchette buzzes under her finger.

Y-O-U-R-F-A-U-L-T.

"Your fault." Valerie repeats, *Your fault*, and there is venom in her voice, and she is looking straight at Alice with her faraway eyes, and Alice moves the planchette with her finger, quickly and forcefully, to GOODBYE.

They are drawing together on the piece of paper. At first their lines had been awkward and separate, Beatrice's resolving into careful loops and the boy's fretful dashes. But now they are in sync, their pencils coming together and moving apart like magnets. They work in silence, the only sound the scratching of their pencils on paper. Alice is at a friend's house, though Beatrice doesn't remember which friend, and she doesn't remember what time she's supposed to be home, and she doesn't know what time it is now. Beatrice can't remember the last time she did this, letting the images come free-form, without censor or model, without measurement or angle. This feeling of lead on paper like skin on skin, an itch you feel along your shoulder blades, the beginnings of wings. When the phone rings, she is startled into consciousness. They both look down at what they've created.

"I never knew God looked like that."

"I think it's my husband," she says.

"You have a husband?"

"He died."

"For your sins?"

The outline of his face on the paper throbs under the living room lights as she walks over to the phone. "Maybe."

James Dean leads Alice into one of the bedrooms of the old house. He asks her to take off her shoes. A streetlight somewhere beyond the window hole provides meager light. Two pristine mattresses are stacked in the middle of the floor. Rain smacks against the floorboards. The smell of wet dust and wood rot. Everyone else has left and it's just the two of them now. Alice's body still buzzes with adrenaline. She doesn't know what exactly happened. Was someone—Valerie?—trying to fuck with her, or was her father really there? Whatever truth the planchette had spelled out, she feels him here beside her now. His wounded expression. His hand on her shoulder so light as to be oppressive. The way he would offer to make her pancakes before he left for work, his voice a little too loud, breath shaky, as if in this one question he was doing battle with all his demons.

After the séance, she'd wanted to go home, hide under a blanket, create a bloody zippered mouth, but then James

Dean grabbed her hand, and something, maybe the ghosts they'd disturbed, urged her to stay. Her feet now on the cold dusty wood. She waits for him to lead her to the mattress, to lay her down gently and take her completely. She is ready. Every moment of her life has been leading here: into oblivion. She imagines each shellacked point of his Mohawk tracing a path down her belly. But he doesn't lead her to the mattress. She follows him to the window, where they both stand barefoot in the slant of rain.

"I lost someone too," James Dean finally says.

So this is what they're supposed to be doing—not searching for ghosts or initiating dark rituals or losing virginities, but sharing their sorrow.

"Winston," he says. "My dog."

Alice turns to look at him, and suddenly James Dean's face is not like James Dean at all, but that of a young silly boy, a dusting of acne along his jaw.

"Hit by a car two months ago. I thought I'd be able to talk to him again."

A familiar yawning inside her chest, a balloon slowly filling with emptiness. Her fingers find the sore on her neck, but it is not enough. James Dean begins to cry, and she leads him to the mattresses.

The voice on the other end of the line is Alice's. Her daughter sounds small and far away. She says she needs a ride. Though Beatrice still feels as if she's moving through some kind of delicious fog, her fingers, still holding the drawing pencil, write down the address on a slip of paper. When Beatrice hangs up, she apologizes to the boy and ushers him out into the world with his pamphlets. It's raining and dark. Inexplicable hours have gone by. He stands on her doorstep like a shunned pet.

"Good luck," Beatrice says to him, and then hurries to her car.

Alice has never called her like this before. She's never gotten into trouble, or been hurt, or let on that she needs anything, really. Even before Alice's father died, she seemed to move through the house, through life, like a thin glittering fish. Her secrets keeping her buoyant and careful. As she drives, either incredibly slow or dangerously fast, she can't tell, through the rainy night, Beatrice imagines over and over leading her daughter into the house, putting a blanket around her shoulders, telling her everything is going to be okay. This is the recurring fantasy of her entire motherhood.

Alice is waiting on the steps of the old house. James Dean stands in the doorway behind her, dejected but maintaining a sense of chivalry. Alice runs into the shelter of the car. They drive in silence. Very slowly in silence. As if her mother is preparing her for something, giving her the time she needs to get ready for what awaits her at the house. There is so much Alice wants to tell her, about the séance and about her father, about what she knows for sure now. Beatrice parks and then opens the door for Alice, takes her by the hand and leads her into the house. The boy is no longer on the front steps. Beatrice can see him off to the right under a streetlamp, dripping with rain, soggy pamphlets clutched in his hands, but she pretends not to.

"Who is that?" Alice asks as her mother fumbles with the keys.

"Who? Oh, I don't know."

"He's staring. Like he knows you."

Inside, she puts a blanket over Alice's shoulders, rubs her back, murmurs into her wet hair that everything is going to be all right. The doorbell rings, but neither makes a move to answer. Alice lets her mother hold her. The buzzing in her bones slows to an ache. When that has subsided, they go into the kitchen, where Beatrice begins making fried chicken from a box. Frozen drumsticks hiss in the hot oil of the pan.

Alice lies on the bathroom floor, a deep gash carved into the smooth skin of her forehead. A line of blood is drawn down the side of her nose to crust darkly at the corner of her mouth. The skin around the wound lifts away in goopy clumps. Her eyes are wide open and staring.

"The blood wouldn't drip that way," Beatrice says. "The angle of your head means it would drip to the side, to the floor."

"What happened when Dad died?" she asks from the floor, trying to move her mouth as little as possible.

"You know what happened. He had a cerebral aneurysm that burst. It happened very quickly."

"Did you call 911 right away?"

"What do you mean?"

"I mean, did you wait a minute, or did you call as soon as you knew something was wrong?"

"I called right away."

"I don't remember you ever kissing, or touching each other."

"We did."

"He resented me."

"What are you talking about? Your father loved you very much."

"Not as much as you did."

"Fathers can't. It's biology."

Alice walks into the kitchen and stands beside her mother, mouth blood-dark and zippered shut. It still pains Beatrice to look at her daughter's perfect skin, marred almost beyond recognition. She's done the zippered mouth for weeks now, and Beatrice has to unzip her to hear her speak. Her teachers have reached out and expressed concern. They usually first offer condolences, say they know it must be difficult after her husband's passing, to raise a daughter amidst all that grief.

She wants to tell them it's not very different from what it's always been. There are simply fewer points to connect. Someday there will no longer be any further permutations, all possible lines from A to B drawn, and then what? Then there will be nothing for any of them to do but erase, wash it off, press delete, and start over.

BESTIARY II: Suburban Fox

This fox is somewhat like his feral cousin and maintains a few of the characteristics that have been exaggerated and glorified in myths and children's cartoons. He is still sly and cunning. He will still kill your chickens, those of you who insist on trying that kind of thing out here, or at least steal their eggs (as long as they're fairly easily accessed; the suburban fox has no patience for complicated wire netting or dogs that bark too loudly). But he also has a certain level of sophistication, one that can only come from the curbside taste of discarded though perfectly fresh seared scallops in a lemongrass crème fraîche and knowing one's way around an organic garden bed, able to discern between a Black Krim Heirloom and a Ponderosa Pink, the ripeness of a Charentais cantaloupe (perfect for a mid-dusk summer snack on a sprinkler-sodden lawn).

If, say, you are walking down the sidewalk, on the way to meet a new lover, heart full of chintzy forevers, song in your head promulgating a childish ideal of romantic love you should have outgrown years ago, humming and admiring the way your sunset-back-lit silhouette sways like you're made entirely of liquid—if at that moment, you happen to see this fox on the opposite side of the street, trotting along like he owns the block, his coat so vibrant and shiny he could be in a movie, please, I implore you: don't attach anything to this. The chances of this spotting are above average. It happens to all of us sooner or later. It does not mean you are special, a sign that this lover and you are the reincarnation of Abelard and Héloïse, or even that you have a particular affinity for animals. Just keep walking. In fact, if you can find a sharp stick or heavy stone, throw that in his general direction—not to do harm, necessarily, but to send a message: this is no place for a wild animal.

Dog Story

Arnie makes his careful way up the walk at a moonless two a.m. on memory and a sliver of lamplight through closed curtains. Laura left the lights on again, every one except the porch light. He goes through the house turning them off: bathroom, living room, kitchen. In each one, he waits until the blinding hot blink fades to shadow.

Nails scrape against wood as Hummingbird tries to raise herself from the bedroom floor. She comes staggering into the dark kitchen and he kneels, buries his face in white fur that smells, lately, like his wetsuit when he hasn't washed it in a while. She's been having trouble getting around, sheds hair by the handful, even in the chill fog. Keeps chewing on herself, left back leg down to raw blood-freckled skin. There have been pills and shots; the cream the vet recommended doesn't seem to do anything but make her throw up after she's licked it off. She's old, Dr. Altman said at their last visit, it's time—skin, intestines, bones. They won't be able to manage her pain for much longer. Arnie tells Laura he isn't stalling; there should just be an intuitive pace for this kind of thing. *Keeping time.* To hold the space between sound. As if any part of time can be captured, owned, set apart from everything else.

"Still my baby," he whispers in her ear, and she licks his nose until he stands.

I know what you're thinking: another story about a dying dog. Just what the world needs. You've heard this one before. But we still cling to pop songs and fairy tales—repetition is what saves us.

Maybe the person who needs saving is me. It makes me uncomfortable to trick you into complicity, and it's not in my nature to ask for things. But between the three of us, the four of us, the ten of us, maybe we can come to an understanding. Arnie will only show us what he wants to show us. We will not sentimentalize. We will follow the breadcrumbs and not ask too many questions. If there is any sand left in the hourglass when we're done, we will split it evenly between us.

Instead of turning the light back on, Arnie opens the cupboard in the dark. It doesn't seem to matter to him these days, clear or brown. He barely looks. He stands at the window and pours some into a glass. It's brown.

Yes, this story is also about an alcoholic musician who's lost his verve. Whose slow emotional decay through the years has formed a crust of stagnation that could be interpreted as contentment if you're not looking too closely. This is a necessary component of the dying dog story: to access the damaged part in each of us, the misunderstood bard we secretly understand.

Fog hovers on all sides of the house in a way it never does in the day. It isolates, mutes, makes everything feel smaller, powerless, private parts bared then ridiculed by their very nature. If he opens the window, Arnie will hear ocean, the steady break of waves two hundred feet from where he stands. But then he'd let that fog all the way in to obliterate the solid pumping things behind his skin he's been working so hard to keep intact. We imagine him opening the window, imagine the fog like something poured, curling its milky tentacles into his ears and eyes and mouth. The mattress groans from down the hall, and we're reminded imagination has nothing to do with this.

Creak of footsteps, and then Laura is behind him. Hands underneath his shirt, hair tickling the backs of his arms. She hasn't been this close, so intimate, in a while. He takes a deep breath of her: the opposite of decay—newly rinsed, recently bloomed. It must require willpower not to push her up against the cupboards, to check the hunger her reserve elicits. The smug, secretive carnality underneath all that flannel.

"How was the show?" she asks, her voice soft with sleep.

"Fine. Same old."

"Did you tell the guys about tomorrow night?"

"Yeah."

"What did they say?"

"Oh, you know. That they'd come. That it was a little morbid. I told 'em it was your idea."

"Ha."

"Did you order the cake?" she asks.

"Yeah. Should be ready for pickup tomorrow after one, they said."

"You didn't have them write anything on it, did you?"

Laura is no different from most of the girls who'd come in and then out of Arnie's life. Thirteen years younger than he, raked with a feral, fidgety beauty. They met at one of his local gigs, where she danced through their entire set, thick dark hair—dreaded in places, braided in others—moving with her like Medusa's snakes. She was in his bed that night, then the next, and she's still there, like the Stones' greatest hits, like "Visions of Johanna" played at the very end of the night, something we hum in our sleep.

"Is this new?" Arnie picks up one of the glass animals from the windowsill: some kind of quadruped, giraffe body with a long tapered elephant trunk. The college let Laura use the furnaces of their glass studio for a nominal monthly fee. Something about her creations makes us sad but horny, their impossible appendages wrought so delicately.

"Yeah. I just finished it. I call it a Giraffant."

"You're getting really good. You know that?"

She circles his wrist with her finger. Her hands are rough with calluses, interrupted by the smooth pink coins of recent burns. When she puts them on him, there must be no mistaking it. Though she's doing less of that. We imagine baptismal shiver across our veins.

She takes the whiskey from his hand and sips, grunting as she hands it back. "God, Arnie, that's like gasoline."

Hummingbird starts to whine. Or maybe she's been whining and we just now notice. These days her whines are high and hushed, like she's trying not to bother anyone.

Laura sits down on the linoleum next to her. The ghosts of her breasts still press beneath our shoulder blades.

"*Faith has been broken, tears must be cried,*" he sings. "*Let's do some living, after we die.*"

Laura strokes Hummingbird's head, rubbing her ears. "Did you call Dr. Altman?"

"You used to love that song."

"Did you set something up?"

"She wasn't there. I left a message."

"When's the last time you wrote one of your own songs?"

"Nobody ever really writes their own songs."

"You're not doing her any favors, Arnie."

"It's my job to sing other people's songs."

Laura sighs and lifts her hand: a tuft of white fur falls from her fingers, to become one of the many spectral tumbleweeds that drift through the house.

"It's raining," she says.

We look out the window. Little more than a drizzle, just enough to make a person feel tired.

-:¦:-

"You guys gonna play?" Luis asks. Hair, eyelashes, eyebrows, skin—all in shades of sand. We can't look at him very long without squinting. Arnie squirts a little more Cheez Whiz in Hummingbird's dish.

"Yeah, later." Arnie pours the last of the Evan Williams into two shot glasses, hands one to Luis, taking it down before Luis has a chance to cheers to something.

"I'm officially putting in a request for 'Honky Tonk Women.' You guys killed it last time."

There were stories about Luis. That he'd lost his wife and kids in a car crash years ago, that he'd been driving drunk. Also that he lived by himself in a sea cave. He collected mermaids. Danced with sharks. He was immortal. These people love their local lore. Arnie never pries. They mostly talk about the waves, or music. Arnie likes him. They share some deep ancestral darkness, both know stuff in their bones that could never be communicated to the rest of these people.

"She's so sweet," Luis says, crouching down. Hummingbird rolls onto her back, reaching a front paw behind her like a reluctant lover.

"She's a little hussy."

"It's the end of an era. That's for sure," Luis says.

"Yeah." Arnie suddenly looks wrung-out. It might be the light, but his skin seems grayish and loose, like he's underwater. He takes a swig from the bottle then hands it to Luis. "She's been with us for a while."

"How are we ever going to find another mascot?"

"That's it for me, I'm afraid."

"Laura said you guys are thinking about Portland."

Laura's been talking about Portland. Oregon. The music scene there, she says, is right up his alley. She thinks the change of pace will be good for them, maybe he can start writing music again, a chance for her to bring her glass animals to a wider audience. He tells her he's been to Portland. Hipsters in skinny jeans and ratty messenger bags, rushing to see whatever tone-deaf experimental group the indie mag reviews favorably that day. He can't imagine leaving Pismo, he says—bright wildflower cliffs slowly crumbling, every day a new profile etched from the loam by wind and salt. His band is here, the house he's lived in for the last ten years. He's been around, he knows something about switching locations.

We watch Chrissy walk over to where Laura's alone contemplating her beer bottle. She says something in Laura's ear. Chrissy and Arnie had a thing before Laura, brief but pretty hot. The day he broke it off, she unbuttoned her shirt and unhooked her bra and pulled down her skirt and then threw a coffee mug at his head—just missed him. They both look over at them and Arnie looks away.

"Portland's got a lot going on. A good place to play music for a real audience."

"I'm kinda particular to the local one."

"You know, sometimes, I look up from one of these parties, and I realize I don't know anyone," Luis says.

"It's my house, and I feel the same way."

"So this one's for old Hummingbird?"

"Yeah. It's weird, right?"

"I don't know. The cake's a little weird. But I get it."

Nobody has touched the cake. White frosting with the outline of a paw and "Goodbye Hummingbird" written across the top.

"You want a piece?"

"No, man."

Arnie locates Laura against the wall talking to John and Pat from next door, microbrew bottle in her hand. She's wearing a short billowy sundress and cowboy boots, dark hair gathered at her neck, bare shoulders.

"You're lucky," Luis says. We think he's referring to Laura, but when Arnie looks over, Luis is looking down at Hummingbird.

"Why?"

"You got to share a whole life and death with another living thing. There aren't other moments of absence that you can regret, chunks of her life you can only imagine."

Arnie looks unsure what they're talking about. The band's drummer, Tony, walks by and points at him with a sloppy grin, and we know it's only a matter of time before the hugging begins.

"I got her from the shelter," Arnie says. He reaches down and gathers some of Hummingbird's fur at her nape. She looks up at him adoringly. "They said she was found on the side of the highway, six weeks old and full of fleas, dehydrated, her ribs showing." He releases and blows a fistful of white hair like dandelion seeds. "It was love at first sight."

Luis crouches and takes Hummingbird's big shaggy head in his hands.

"A lucky dog."

⁓

No matter how much whiskey he drinks, Arnie doesn't seem to be getting drunk. In his head, he'd probably pictured this whole thing differently. A celebration, a chance for Hummingbird to feel good and loved before leaving this world. But nobody is very interested in Hummingbird. This is just another gathering, some young people, some old, long flowing skirts and torn jeans, pierced, tattooed, tan people with knots in their hair, scars and chapped lips, the beach people, the ones who stay through the bare bones of tourist-less winter, who surf in 12°C, who make pottery and seashell jewelry and kombucha and store it all for summer like bears. They think this party is for them, a way to ward off the shivering fog, to relieve the restlessness of empty cafés.

He reaches down and grabs Hummingbird's dish, rinsing out the untouched Cheez Whiz in the sink.

"A pretty good turnout," Laura says, suddenly right beside him, before there's time to prepare.

"I guess." He pours two shots and hands one to her.

Laura leans down and rubs Hummingbird behind her ears, eliciting a grumbled, half-broken moan. "This was your idea."

"I know."

"Arnie, she's in a lot of pain." Laura looks up at him and shakes her head.

"I know."

She straightens and steps closer to Arnie. Her nose almost touches his lips, and we feel that familiar ache in his chest. "I don't understand you," she says. "I know you don't want her to suffer."

He pushes his lips against hers. Someone starts to play his bongo drums in the corner, the beat dumb and knotted. He opens his mouth. Drinks her, beer and honey.

"I'm sorry," she says. She takes a step back. The whiskey is finally catching up, we see it in his face, a warm splotchy flush, too-hard gaze, like everything is moving through something else.

"It's OK," he says, slurring his words a bit. "I get it."

The voices and laughter have risen a notch, which strangely makes it feel like we're all alone.

"I'm glad one of us does," Laura says. She looks down at Hummingbird. "I think I need a walk."

Hummingbird lifts her eyes at the word. Arnie doesn't look able to move from his place in the kitchen.

"OK," he says.

He helps Hummingbird up and they walk slowly outside, past the people smoking and laughing in the front yard, people who slap Arnie on the back and touch Laura's bare arm, crouch and pat Hummingbird's back. They walk down the sidewalk to the water and as they reach the sand, there's a noticeable change in temperature. Hummingbird crouches and strains to pee, looking up at them in embarrassed pain. It's misty and sunless. Nobody else is on the beach. Arnie takes his jacket off and wraps it around Laura's shoulders. They walk a little further down the sand and then Laura takes off her shoes and sits. Lumps of seaweed vibrate with flies. Arnie sits beside her and they both watch as Hummingbird catches up and settles in front of them, an ordeal of digging in the sand, turning around, shifting one hip down and then the other. She settles in with a high taut whine.

"I do love this place," Laura says, as if continuing an earlier discussion.

"I do too."

The tide is low, and black-capped terns dot the darker patted-down sand. Some of them are sitting, heads tucked into feathers, as if waiting for the fish to come to them.

"Can you imagine the first time someone discovered glass? That you could light the sand on fire," she says. Arnie tries to look at her, but seems to find it difficult to keep his neck turned like that in the cold. One of the birds walks slowly up to another one and settles down directly behind it.

"What is more beautiful than a window?" she asks.

Arnie looks sick. He probably should have eaten something.

"It won't change anything," he says.

A wave crashes, much bigger than the previous ones. The tide's coming back in, but the terns don't move.

"I don't want it to."

Arnie looks at her and she smiles, in that wistful way of someone who's already made up her mind. "I made you something," she says.

Laura reaches into the pocket of her coat and takes out a wad of newspaper. He takes it from her and carefully unwraps it. He studies the arch and bump of colorless glass. We can't make heads or tails of it. Though there definitely is some kind of head and some kind of tail.

"It's a Wom-ine," she says, grinning. And we can sort of see it now, the woman's face featureless, but an intimation of hair, breasts. Canine legs and tail.

"I thought you never do humans."

"Yeah, well, I made an exception."

"Thanks." This was the first one she'd ever made expressly for him. He should probably feel flattered, but we don't exactly know what it's supposed to mean. Is it a riddle or a gift? He holds it in his palm.

"*Yes, how many years can a mountain exist, before it's washed to the sea? Yes, how many years can some people exist, before they're allowed to be free?*" he sings—charmingly, we think, but Laura doesn't seem moved. She stares out at the water.

He reaches over and puts his hand on Hummingbird's back, letting it rise and fall with her breath. "She doesn't have any trouble breathing," he says.

"That doesn't mean she's not in pain."

He takes his hand from Hummingbird and puts it over

Laura's in the sand.

"The fog's coming in," she says, and all of a sudden she's right. The fog spreads a dense shadow an inch above the water. The seagull begins to eat something it's found in the sand, and a few of the other birds turn to watch him.

Back at the house, a crowd is gathered in the living room. The music and laughter have stopped. Hummingbird begins to whine again and Arnie picks her up. She takes up his entire torso. There is someone, a body, on the floor in the center of the crowd.

"Is he breathing?" Arnie asks. A couple people turn to look at him like he's not the one who lives here. He comes closer and we realize it's Luis. Someone is giving him CPR.

"Hey, that's Luis," he says.

"Do you know him?"

"Yeah." Doesn't everyone?

He catches Laura's eye on the other side of the crowd. Beautiful in her worry. Hand at her neck, she looks at him like he should do something. He probably should do something. Hummingbird puts her dog head on his shoulder, and he presses his cheek against her fur. She makes a noise in her throat like she, for once, is glad to be alive.

He puts her down outside the circle, a spot far enough away that people won't accidentally step on her but not so far that she can't see him. He comes closer to Luis. The crowd parts, ready for someone to make sense of things.

And there he is, what doesn't so much look like Luis anymore. It's him, but a version we haven't seen—a hanging wide open. A body at the end of a sandstorm. Arnie crouches and the sirens get louder.

The guy who was giving him CPR is still sitting on the floor. He looks at Arnie.

"Is he a friend of yours?"

"He's dead," Arnie says. Probably *friend* was inadequate. Arnie couldn't tell anyone where Luis lives or his last name, but he could talk about his fear of bees, in particular being trapped in a bathroom with one, or what he would say about the mustache—too groomed, too pretentiously ironic—CPR guy was rocking.

"He's not dead," CPR guy says.

Luis is moving, moving and breathing. His eyes are glazed over and he's coughing, but he's alive.

"Hey buddy, just hang on, try not to move too much, paramedics will be here any second," CPR says.

Luis closes his eyes. Despite the instructions, he turns over on his side and hugs his knees. A gesture of embarrassment maybe. Arnie stands to give his friend some room. He finds Hummingbird where he left her and picks her up again. People are already starting to break up, walk away. Lights flash through the windows. Someone lets the paramedics in.

A flurry of clearing space, lifting, vitals called, and then Luis is floating through the air on a gurney, then gone. The paramedics have left the back door open, and we watch Arnie watch Laura cross the kitchen to close it. She walks with her head down, arms hugging her chest. As she shuts the door and turns around, he tries to put Hummingbird down, but she starts to whine again. To reach out— that's all it would take, a few steps, an extended arm, and he could pull her to him—but the CPR guy walks up and starts asking him questions, and she's gone again, talking to someone on the other side of the room.

"You know that guy? Is he a friend of yours? Who was he here with?"

Arnie shrugs. "I think he came by himself. His name

is Luis."

"Someone should go with him to the hospital."

A group begins to gather, seeming to accept without question their next move, quickly exiting together out the back door as if they'd rehearsed it beforehand. Laura is part of this group. She already has on her coat and a bright red wool hat.

He catches her eye. Stay, he mouths.

What? she mouths back. The cold wet air comes in, and Hummingbird begins to shiver in his arms.

"He just crumpled to the floor," a girl beside us is saying. "He was standing there one minute, and then the next he was out."

"Stay," he says now, out loud. "Stay."

But Laura shakes her head with impatience. She runs over, breathless.

"We're going to try to find someone," she says. "There has to be someone, he must have people here somewhere." She puts her hand on Hummingbird.

"Where are you going to look?"

"I don't know. Chrissy thinks he used to date her neighbor."

"That sounds rock solid."

Laura presses her lips together in a clear sign of annoyance and pets Hummingbird.

"I'm sorry," he says. "How are you doing?"

"Me? I'm fine. I mean, it's sad. It's weird, isn't it? What do you think happened?"

"I don't know. I guess we'll find out."

"You were talking to him earlier. How did he seem?"

"Normal. A little buzzed, I guess, but fine."

She takes her hand from Hummingbird and briefly sets it on his shoulder.

"I'll call you and let you know what we find out. You sure you don't want to come?"

"I wasn't asked."

"Do you want to come?"

He looks around. "No. I should stay here. I should stay with her." He shifts Hummingbird in his arms. It must be painful, his arms must feel like they're about to fall off. But this is all he has left, this mute martyrdom, this small sacrifice.

A car honks outside. "I gotta go," she says. She gives him a peck on the cheek, waves, then closes the door behind her. The few people who remain in the kitchen are looking at him. He puts Hummingbird down.

"What's wrong with your dog?" someone asks, a young guy we've seen hanging around. Baseball cap, a white shirt like a garbage bag, like he's all bones underneath. There seem to be more and more of these young people lately, this whole group of weird kids suddenly everywhere, waiting to take over.

"Nothing's wrong with her."

Hummingbird stays where he puts her down, on her belly on the linoleum. She starts to whine.

"Are you sure? I think something might be wrong."

"She's dying."

"Geez. Sorry, man."

Arnie starts to clear the empty bottles and cups. Most everyone has left. A few stragglers in the living room, but their noise is muffled, far away. There was talk of another party, one without a dying dog and a body on the floor.

What could have happened to Luis? we wonder. He couldn't have been older than Arnie. Fifty was pushing it. Maybe he had a condition. After all, nobody really knew him. At least, not that we know of. But maybe he just had too much to drink; a close call. Maybe you shouldn't taunt death, like once you talk about it in the open, welcome it with cake, bad things happen. Does Arnie consider his own mortality? Is he thinking about the randomness of loss, his own culpability in what he gives up and what he dials in? He's not giving us anything.

Arnie reaches into the pocket of his jeans and pulls out the glass Wom-ine. The tail has broken off. It looks almost like a normal human woman now. He holds the two pieces of glass in his palm. There's a thing he should be doing, we think, a moment that should be observed. A prayer. He sets the pieces of glass on the windowsill and opens the window. Fog seeps in like a living mass. It covers everything, obscuring even his hand in front of his face. Okay so it's not that thick, but we like to imagine the fog doing something for once, uncoiling inside him, removing blood and organs, washing everything out. Hummingbird's whine is the only thing that makes it through. A thin line of pain, desire, dreams, panic, song. The only thing reliable, his foundation. But where is Hummingbird?

Arnie looks in the living room, the bedroom, the back-yard. He asks everyone still there if they've seen her, but none of them have. He continues to call her name, though the whining has stopped. He tells everyone to be quiet. He tells everyone to leave.

He checks under the bed and in the crawlspace underneath the stairs. He's not crying so much as moaning from his solar plexus. It's not hard to imagine Hummingbird dragging herself off somewhere, wanting one last final moment of peace, shivering in the cold, retching from the pain. We know this is what Arnie is imagining, the recognition he will soon find her body, that he will have failed to share with her, to comfort, in her final moment. If he can just get to her in time, maybe he can save her. But we also know this isn't going to happen. We knew from the start a dog was going to die. Arnie circles the house and then walks down to the sand and sits down. There's no moon, and he waits for his eyes to adjust to the dark.

This is like a recurring dream we have. The occasion changes, but there's always an ocean nearby, and it's only the last minute that we're able to go to it, we almost miss the opportunity. The water is clear and beautiful and we stare into it, hoping to see something. And because we hope, and it is our dream after all, things start to appear—a bloated purple starfish from someone else's childhood, a zebra running along the ocean floor, a killer whale holding a grudge from another dream we can't quite remember—and we don't know what to do with it, all this strange and terrible beauty. So we just walk away, and then we wake up.

Arnie stares into the sky, starless and so much like nothing it would be difficult to call it black. He just stares and stares, and we're not sure what he's looking for or if he's finding it. He begins to sing a song, a song we've heard before, everyone's heard this song, but it doesn't matter to him, he continues, sings it as if it's his song, rising from his gut teeming with sand and stars and dog-hair tumbleweeds. We stay and listen for as long as we can. It's the least we can do.

BESTIARY III: Attic Raccoon

Raccoons are notorious suburban pests. They get into trash, eat cat food, demolish carefully planted vegetable gardens. They are known to carry rabies. Often they will settle in attics or other tightly enclosed spaces, which they compromise—break wood beams, eviscerate boxes of old photographs.

Understandable why a responsible homeowner would want to get rid of these animals. And there are numerous resources: specialists one can hire to capture, kill, relocate, techniques for deterrence involving loud noises and lights. I won't go into detail here. But I would like to point out what you may not know—that almost two thirds of the area of the raccoon's cerebral cortex dedicated to sensory perception is specialized for the tactile, more than in any other animal. Whisker-like hairs on their hypersensitive front paws help them discern the minutest physical nuance. The pickpockets and origamists of the animal world.

When I think of these creatures, I am reminded of our own Tom Keenan. If you're not already familiar with the story: Tom recently returned from his fifth year in Afghanistan. Hadn't wanted to go in the first place; did it for the money, tuition, benefits. But then when it came time for him to be released, he had some trouble adjusting to civilian life. He said that when he was home, with his wife and two little girls, this family he'd worked so hard to create—for whom he did it all, to make sure they had a good life—he couldn't get back to the man he was. He'd seen too much:

exploding limbs, children sailing through the air like Fris-
bees. Killed. Felt the wild pumping of his heart dispense a
hatred not his own.

Back home, the littlest tasks required tremendous effort:
buying paper towels at the grocery store, sticking the stamp
on a letter. Every color became a taste, each smell a sound.
His world transformed into a carnival fun house of stim-
ulation. The last straw, he said, was one day after picking
up his kids from school. At the McDonald's drive thru, he
closed his fingers around a greasy bag of Chicken McNug-
gets and the whole world folded in on itself. His two little
girls became human-shaped hums, the boy at the window
sharp and tangy, pickled ginger, the window itself stench
of Back Bay, nothing behind his own eyelids but dusty twi-
light blue. He crawled into the backseat under a blanket
until his wife was able to come get them.

Tom ended up digging a big hole in his backyard, where
he now lives. His wife and kids communicate with him
mostly through walkie-talkies, and they hand him food
and exchange jars of waste through a bucket-pulley system.
In a radio interview aired last Sunday, his voice static and
echo, he said he felt much better. This earth is where we
come from and where we'll return.

The family has asked me to relate something to you: Tom
is not a prophet. Please stop throwing your scraps of ques-
tions and requests for predictions over the Keenans' fence.
Some of them have been falling into the hole, and for Tom,
they are saxophonic burnt popcorn supernovas. It takes his
family days to clear the space and get him back to zero.

The First Location

The girl had been in Shannon's English class, indistinguishable before she went missing from the others. The ones chiseled from marble, spun from silk. They walked around campus like gods holding their power in check, gracious with omniscience. They sat beside her in lecture halls, in classrooms with tidy rows of desks, and mostly acted like she didn't exist. She was an uncomfortable reminder, a specter, the Ghost of Female Future. Yes, her presence said— one day, and it will happen before you know it, these lines around your eyes, this splintering of beauty. Your hair will lose its gloss. The bagger at the grocery store calls you ma'am. The construction workers let you pass by in peace. You walk down the street trying not to think about your own body, your twenty-year-old self living inside you like another beating heart.

On the small TV above the bar, they showed the same picture they always showed: The missing girl against a tree in a park, straight white teeth, long blond hair pulled off a pretty neck. Looking as if she'd just received an award, or fallen in love.

The story still ran periodically, though it had been almost three months now and no new information had been found. How tragedy struck a small Midwestern college town last March when a young girl disappeared while walking home alone. Over images of street corners and dry empty fields, the newscaster recited details in a blunt unmusical tone. The missing girl's cell phone found in the grass by the Walmart just outside town, the only fingerprints her own, no outgoing calls or texts past the time she went missing. Friends say she'd left the bar early, that it was not yet dark, that she didn't have far to go. A walk they'd all done before, down streets considered safe enough. The story continued to offer up the missing girl's bland credentials—on the volleyball team, a straight-A student, reliable teammate and friend, kind daughter and sister, a delightful student!—intended as clues or warnings, breadcrumbs for the rest of them to follow. But where, Shannon wondered. Out of danger, or into it?

One was expected to be prepared, remain vigilant, in a constant state of caution and suspicion—but maybe, Shannon thought, there was nothing better than dissolving into thin air.

The bartender pointed his finger at her, and she nodded. She'd forgotten his name but felt like he might know her better than most people. Besides the two or three locals who enjoyed day drinking, the bar was often empty at this hour. Today there was only one other person, and he'd chosen the seat next to her, so close she could smell the booze on his breath. Students came at the end of the night for strong pours and cheap shots, but it didn't have much atmosphere. No jukebox or video games or pool table. Just a bar and some hard wooden stools.

"These girls," the man said now, shaking his head. "They think they're invincible."

It took her a moment to realize he was referring to the missing girl, though she wondered why he spoke in the plural. Perhaps it was their collective fault, a responsibility all girls shouldered together.

"It's awful," she said, trying to sound private, dismissive.

"I bet he's got her somewhere." He looked up at the screen and nodded. "She's probably just down the street, right under everyone's noses, chained to a radiator in the basement." He grinned at her. He had heavy-lidded eyes, a glazed-over hunger in them that suggested pharmaceuticals and arrogance. A few years younger than Shannon, mid-thirties maybe, and overdressed in an old-fashioned way: navy blazer, a gauzy yellow handkerchief in the breast pocket. She'd never seen him at the bar before, though the bartender had said his name, *Bennett, Bennie,* as way of greeting.

She briefly considered whether he could be a kidnapper. Too clean, she decided, too comfortable with himself. Those guys, the predators, they usually had a quirk, a tic, they gave their depravity away by how they weren't in complete control of their body's mechanics. She made a sound that was neither agreement nor dismissal.

"'He seemed like such a nice guy,' his neighbors will say. 'Always trimming his rosebushes and walking his little Pomeranian.'" He removed a roll of breath mints from his pocket and offered her one.

"No, thank you," she said, and that seemed to be all the encouragement he needed.

"What's a nice girl like you doing in a place like this?" he said, and, "You've got beautiful eyes," and, later, "It's rare to meet a woman with looks and brains these days." There was an ironic playfulness in his delivery that made it clear both that he was hitting on her and that he knew how creepy that was. She appreciated the honesty in this approach, what seemed to her the only real way to do it these days. And it was good to have a drinking partner.

Sometimes she brought her homework to the bar, or to Bennett's. He lived over someone else's garage. Hardwood floors and shabby oriental rugs, amateur watercolors of ships handsomely framed. She didn't get much work done either place, but she did get drinking done. Though she and Bennett really had nothing in common, they had that, and they had the other thing. There was a balcony off his living room that overlooked a pool where the house's children frolicked. Cries of *Marco* and *Polo* sometimes masked her own noises. They would sit outside when the pool was still and quiet, drink vodka tonics and nurture their own private thoughts. She knew it wasn't love, but it was nice to be with someone without judgment. Bennett had many flaws, but he never made her feel bad about herself.

And they had the missing girl.

It started when he picked her up one day wearing a ski mask. When she laughed and tried to tug it off, he told her to shut up, and when they got to his place, they couldn't find the bed fast enough. They'd since incorporated rope and duct tape.

"I've been watching you."

"Please don't hurt me."

"That's enough talking, little girl."

Sometimes he left her in the apartment tied to the bed for hours at a time. There was a delirium she fell into, a fugue state between lucidity and dreaming, desire and repulsion. She lay there staring up at the ceiling, her movement restricted, her mind free of the daily hum of guilt and inadequacy.

"Marco!" she would shout down to the kids in the pool, but they never responded.

"That's sick, Shannon," Maya said. "What's happened to you?"

On the phone to her sister, she tried to explain without it seeming too weird. They'd never been particularly close but had maintained the practice of weekly phone calls since their mother died. It was clear both of them saw these calls as a chore to get through, but the chore was better than the guilt.

"Nothing's happened to me. I'm just having some fun. Aren't I allowed to have fun?"

But that wasn't the complete truth. It wasn't fun, exactly. It was necessary. Like jumping up and down when you're cold. Moving something that needed moving.

"This is like some weird midlife crisis. It's weird, Shannon."

Her sister had always held her at a distance, like a goldfish in a bowl. She would peer into the glass from time to time to make sure Shannon was still alive and to congratulate herself on not being a goldfish.

"I shouldn't have said anything," Shannon said.

"Where is Eric during all of this?"

"Oh, he watches, but doesn't participate."

"Shannon!"

"I never bring him to the house. And Eric's been spending most of his time at his father's anyway."

Her sister sighed, and there were sounds of movement. Shannon imagined her with the phone cradled between her shoulder and ear, making dinner while helping her kids with their homework and mopping the floor and looking amazing while doing it.

"Are you drinking?" her sister asked.

"I'm having a glass of wine. Is that a crime?"

"Yes. In some countries it is."

"What happened?" Bennett asked one night, after, as they were lying in his bed. Her wrists were still tied to the bedpost, though he'd released her feet, and she wrapped her legs around him. He traced the scar along her cheekbone.

After six months, it had mostly healed but there was still a faint white line.

"Car accident," she said. And he didn't ask anything more, but she told him anyway. How she ran a red light, how when she looked at it she swore it was yellow, how she remembered singing at the top of her lungs to some stupid pop song, then headlights and glass. Her son was saved by his seatbelt, but somehow his leg got caught when the car flipped, his tibia fractured. She survived completely unscathed. The tibia took months to heal, months Eric struggled with crutches, zoned out on pain meds. He could no longer play football. How she had been drinking. Not much, but enough.

"Does he blame you?"

"What do you think?"

"Maybe the light was yellow."

She shook her head in the dark.

Saturday night, one of her weekends with Eric, she waited up for him, watching a show on TV called *Vanished* and mixing generous vodka tonics. It was some kind of marathon. Ever since the girl's disappearance, it seemed like they were all over the place, the stories of the missing. People exchanged them at the bar and the store and at school. Friends of friends, second cousins, old childhood playmates. Jimmy Hoffa. D. B. Cooper. Errol Flynn's son. Mystery gave weight to the details of their lives in a way death never could. Speculation kept them alive. Amelia Earhart flying over the Pacific—crashed her plane on a deserted island and lived the rest of her days tangled in seaweed with Fred Noonan, drinking the milk of coconuts and catching fish with her bare hands.

On the show the saddest ones were those whose case

was still open, mystery never solved. The fathers who went out every day to search for their long lost daughters. The despair on their faces, voices cracking—stuck in limbo, able to neither grieve nor rejoice.

She waited until Eric's curfew, and then an hour later, and then another hour. He wasn't responding to her texts. When he finally walked through the door, she forgot to be grateful.

"Where were you? You were supposed to be home two hours ago."

"Sorry, sorry, I know," he said, shedding his coat like a weary father after a long day of work. He towered over her by a good six inches now. "We were at this party, and Tyler had too much to drink, and I kept trying to get him to leave with me, but he wouldn't, and I didn't want to abandon him. I was going to call, but I didn't want to wake you."

"Have you been drinking?" she asked.

"Not really. I had one beer. I see you have, though."

"Sit down," she said.

He perched on the edge of the couch and sighed.

"What's going on?"

"What do you mean?" He brushed the long bangs from his forehead with a gesture that made him seem much older than his seventeen years. She wondered when his last haircut was. It got confusing with him spending so much time with his father, in whose domain things fell.

"We never get to just talk anymore. I don't know what's going on with you."

"What are you watching?"

She'd forgotten about the show. On the screen a young man had his arm around a crying older woman.

"Oh I don't know, some show about missing persons."

"Jesus, Mom."

"What?"

"Can't you watch something a little more upbeat?"

She looked at the TV. A reenactment now: headlights coming upon a lone woman on a dark street.

"It's interesting," she said. "These people, they never see it coming."

He looked at her, a flicker of something she couldn't read. "I'm tired," he said, rising and climbing the stairs before she could think of something to make him stay. A slight limp from the accident that he tried to hide. He used the banister for support.

She didn't want to admit that it was easier when he wasn't there. During the weeks he was at his father's, she could breathe easier. Of course she looked forward to his visits, but they'd begun to loom, to cast a shadow. There were too many pieces of him kept from her, chunks of absence that required a closing off to protect from unremitting heartache.

She climbed the stairs. His door was closed, soft beats vibrating out. She knocked softly. When he didn't answer, she knocked louder. She turned the doorknob. He was sitting on his bed, phone in his hand.

"What?" he said. Her heart beat fast. She felt like she'd walked into a stranger's house. There was a poster tacked to the wall of a woman in a skimpy bikini, a Union Jack hung big-bellied from the ceiling, dry erase board with a drawing of a marijuana leaf and some jagged text—*no you don't see me I got moves like beef jerky I love bitches like Obama pardons turkeys.*

"You are my son. This is my house."

"Please," he said, and there was real pleading behind it. "I have to get some sleep."

She failed her algebra exam. Her lit professor had given her an extension for the midterm essay, but it was now due the day after tomorrow and she hadn't even started it. She had rope burns on her wrists, a perpetual tape rash above her lip.

The thrill was beginning to fade. It no longer felt like a forbidden narrative they were exploring together. When Bennett left her tied up, she couldn't stop thinking about all the minutes that were being taken up. All the time she was just a body, existing.

On the phone with her sister, she no longer spoke of Bennett. When asked about school or Eric, Shannon gave answers that were not false.

"Fine," she said. "Everything is fine."

At the spa, a client came in for a deep tissue massage. Usually Carrie, one of the other masseuses, did these, but she was on vacation, and so Shannon had agreed to take over some of her appointments. If she wasn't doing schoolwork, she should at least try to make some money.

The client was a woman around Shannon's age, well manicured and perfumed, hair stiff and precise in a platinum blond bob, thick makeup. Her name *Calista* or *Tamara* or *Melanie*. This was the spa's main clientele. Shannon felt comfortable with these women. She knew what they wanted. Someone to listen to them, someone to feel superior to. To work out all the stress and worry they keep hidden beneath their skin, touch them without judgment.

This one was chatty. She wasted no time in getting to the personal details. Shannon zoned in and out with periodic sounds of response and encouragement as she pressed the heel of her hand between the woman's shoulder blades. Calista was telling a story about someone she was dating, a recent trip. The face rest made it seem as if she were speaking from the bottom of a well.

Being a massage therapist wasn't something Shannon ever saw herself doing for this long. She'd become certified because she thought it would be good experience for nursing school, to get to know the human body, its ligaments and pressure points. But she surprised herself with how much she liked it, how good she was. There was a way in which, after the first couple minutes, as she went deeper into a myofascial trigger point, she would enter a door and the body on the table would open itself to her, her hands moving with a logic she wasn't quite conscious of, a secret language pressed into the muscles, the deep intuitive conversation of flesh, and something like swimming in the ocean would settle in, a sweet churning surrender. Mostly she could separate this from her own desire. But sometimes the urge was too great, the door would open and she would fall in.

"The sex is mind-blowing. I mean, you wouldn't believe," Calista was saying. "So we're going at it, he has me up against a wall, and my friend Veronica knocks on the door." Shannon's right hand began to cramp. This happened from time to time, an inevitable byproduct of doing this work for as long as she had. She shook it out, rolled her wrist, and tried to press through.

"I recently started seeing someone new myself," she said, to try to stop the woman from going where her current anecdote was headed.

"Oh yeah?" she said. "That's wonderful."

She asked the woman to turn over and held the sheet over her.

"It's still pretty new."

"That's the best part. What does he do?"

With her left hand Shannon dug into a lymphatic pressure point in the armpit while lifting the woman's arm with her right.

He ties me up. Presses his knee into my groin until I'm begging.

"He works for the hospital," she said. "Administration stuff." Though she realized she had no idea what he did for a living. Bennett was free most afternoons. Despite his ludicrous outfits, he never seemed to be coming from or going to anywhere in particular. The first time she'd asked he said he was a performance artist, but she didn't believe him.

Suddenly the woman was crying. Tears ran silently from the corners of her closed eyes, which quickly evolved into loud convulsive sobs.

"I'm sorry," Shannon said, gently laying her arm beside her. "Sometimes these pressure points, they release things."

She sat up on the table, the sheet falling away. Shannon tried not to look at her breasts, but they were startling. Pale and flawless, the areolae soft pink shadows of perfect pouty nipples.

"I hate this," the woman said, waving her hand in a gesture that seemed to indicate the whole of her. "It's so terrible growing old. It's so terrible to be at the mercy of your body."

Shannon agreed and handed the woman a tissue.

"You have beautiful breasts," she said. The woman blew her nose and smiled.

"Hi, hot stuff." Bennett sat down next to her at the bar and immediately slid his hand up her thigh, dapper and lecherous as ever in a gray high-collared dress shirt, gold cravat, black wool bowler hat.

"Look at you," she said.

"You like? It came with a feather, but I thought that was a little much."

He looked at her as if he were measuring her for something. She'd bought a short black dress, the kind of thing she never wore. When she saw it on the mannequin, despite her best efforts, she'd immediately thought of this hand on her thigh.

"So I'd like to take you out tomorrow night," he said. "A special date. A surprise." And there was that grin again, not exactly kind, only partially playful.

"I don't think I can do this anymore."

"Can't do what?"

She looked at the book she'd brought with her. She had a test tomorrow and hadn't even cracked it.

"This." She pushed the air between them back and forth.

"What is this?"

"Exactly."

"Well, that's up to you, I guess. But I'm telling you, you're not gonna want to miss it." He looked around the bar, his hand leaving her thigh.

"Fine. Where do you want to meet?"

"The Walmart."

The bartender set a new drink in front of her but didn't look her in the eye. She could feel the judgment coming off him like heat.

"The Walmart? No thank you."

"Fine." He looked at his watch, ran his hand over his hat.

"What time?"

"Seven." He unrolled a breath mint but didn't offer her one.

"Inside?"

"Out front."

"Where are we going?"

"A surprise." He lifted his eyebrows and tilted back on the stool, his hands behind his head.

"What should I wear?"

"Something warm."

-:::-

She wasn't expecting anyone to be there when she got home from the bar, but she turned the corner and Eric was in the kitchen pouring milk over cereal.

"Why aren't you at school?" she asked. "Or at your dad's?"

"It's a holiday. Memorial Day, I think."

"No it's not."

"What's with the dress?"

"It's new. You like it?"

"It's a little early for a dress like that."

"It's noon," she said.

"Hey, Mom, can I ask you something?"

She straightened her shoulders and nodded. She'd only had two vodka tonics but they'd been strong ones.

"Why are you going back to school?"

This was not the question she had expected.

"To try something new," she said, trying to recover. "To try and do something different with my life."

"But why now?" he asked. He looked genuinely interested. She wasn't used to this kind of attention from him.

"It was time." She thought she knew what he was asking, but she didn't know how to answer. She tried to measure her words but they came out wrong, stilted.

He tipped the bowl to his mouth and drank down the rest of the milk. The Adam's apple she'd never noticed before moved beneath his skin.

"I love you," she said. She looked into his eyes, this person that came from her own body, whose thoughts and feelings she couldn't fathom, couldn't touch, and she wanted so badly to wrap her arms around him, just hold him to her, but she knew he would never allow that. "Do you know that?"

"Love you too," he said. He put the empty bowl in the sink and wiped his mouth with the back of his hand.

"Do you mean it?" she asked.

"I gotta go." He gave her a quick hug, grabbed his backpack by the door, and left. "I mean it," he shouted before he shut the door.

There were hundreds of cars in the Walmart parking lot when she pulled up. A line of cars backed up waiting to get in, an attendant managing traffic and signaling where to go. A huge sign, "Candlelight Vigil for Elizabeth Prufer," stood in front of the lot with a picture of the missing girl. The picture was the same one they kept showing on the news, by now familiar to everyone. Seeing her name felt strange after all this time thinking of her only as the missing girl.

She wondered if Bennett had known about the vigil or if it was just a coincidence. She couldn't remember the last time she'd read a newspaper or gotten her news from anywhere but the snippets she caught on the TV above the bar.

She tried calling him, but he didn't answer. Maybe he was already there, out on the field. A golden sea, all those candles flickering and moving in all those human hands. Slowly she inched forward with the others. She parked and followed the crowd out onto the field. There were volunteers handing out candles and she took one, slim, white, with a paper skirt to catch the wax. Faces crowded together, bodies moving like magnets. Some people were crying, holding onto each other for support. Others were smiling and talking as if this were just another social engagement. She tried looking for Bennett but couldn't find him. A young girl of seven or eight held out her candle to Shannon, pale face on the brink of a terrible adult understanding, and she touched her wick to the girl's flame.

A group was singing on the stage, something high and sweet Shannon didn't recognize. They knew the words by heart and their voices joined together and swooped up and out like a sad beautiful sail.

After the singing, the group stepped off the stage and someone else stepped up, and everyone became quiet. It was the missing girl's father. Shannon recognized him from the news. A lean careful man who wore his sadness like a cape.

He thanked everyone for being there, commended the singers, and then he talked about his family's heartbreak. How every day was a mixture of hope and despair. He asked for a moment of silence. For an observance of her light, of the light that refuses to be snuffed out, the light that will bring her home. Shannon held up her candle with the rest of them, and as quiet fell, she was surprised at the emotion that overtook her. A sky blurred above where the stars used to be, candles flickered, no sound but the occasional sniffle. Separate private souls putting wishes into the night. The missing girl was all of theirs, and time was being stolen, from her, from them. They had to take it back.

She felt herself levitating for a moment, rising above everyone and looking down. Though she was still there, huddled with the rest on the ground. Together they were an ocean of flame. They were particles of light. A pulsating, flickering heap of atoms. Together they could build cities, make art, ease suffering, fight evil.

The missing girl's father thanked them again for coming, and like that it was over. She flew back into her body. People began to walk back to the parking lot. Some of them walked with their candles still lit and others blew them out. There were two large receptacles where the discarded ones went.

Shannon moved with the crowd. She was grateful for them, for the easy way they moved. Her body felt light, buzzing. Her phone buzzed. It was Bennett.

Parking lot. Right side, the text said.

Bennett's little red Honda rounded the corner and turned into the parking lot. People were beginning to get back into their cars. She knew she should be angry, but her heart still felt full. She smiled and waved while still holding the lit candle with her other hand.

He pulled up beside her. He was wearing a black ski mask, just his eyes and mouth showing. Something glinted on the seat next to him. A young couple walked past them, the woman staring at her.

"Get in," he said, in a voice she didn't recognize, a new one, low and menacing. And she did.

Anatomy Is Destiny

They're everywhere. One hummingbird buzzes my head as I step out of the car. Another, seconds later, flies so close to my ear I have to reach out and grab onto Doug's arm to keep from falling down the stairs.

"Don't worry," Doug says. "They're harmless." He sweeps his arm over my head, protective and authoritative, and we manage to make it inside without mishap.

"Would you like a cocktail?" I ask Doug after unpacking a few things. I lean against the doorframe. "We've got stuff for martinis."

"It's two in the afternoon." He sits on the couch, feet up on the glass coffee table.

When Doug told me about this place, he said he'd heard of it through another lawyer at the firm: quiet and tranquil, a real getaway. But now he just sits there, not curious what the backyard is like or where the bedroom is. It occurs to me he's stayed in this condo before.

"Yes, but we're on vacation," I say. I try to be coy. Pout a little, clutch at the doorframe and angle my hip provocatively. "On vacation, we can make up our own cocktail hour." I see the hummingbirds through the glass door, slender buzzing shadows that flit back and forth by the palm tree on the patio. Perhaps it's just one hummingbird, eating and retreating, but it seems like there's an entire league out there.

"Why don't you just sit down for a minute?" he asks. "I

think we should just sit here for a minute and relax."

There's too much synaptic firing to sit. I'm on vacation! I lean against the wall and jiggle my leg, a habit left over from junior high, when I shot up a foot taller than all the boys in one year and my limbs tried to find distraction. The hummingbirds vibrate the windows.

"*Anatomy is destiny*," they say.

I look at Doug. "Did you hear that?"

He scrunches up his eyes. "I said why don't you sit down for a minute. You're making me nervous."

I feel his irritation, starting in my toes and working its way up to my throat.

"What are you doing?" He asks.

"Nothing."

"What are you humming?"

"I'm not humming."

"Are you OK?"

"I'm antsy." I begin to unbutton my sweater. He looks at me like I'm see-through, like he's counting my ribs to make sure they're all there. I let the sweater hang open, let him look at me like that for another second, and then turn around and enter the kitchen. I pour myself some vodka on ice with lots of olive juice and three olives. I use almost half a jar of olive juice.

⁂

When Doug called to ask me to go away with him for the weekend, I panicked at first. Things had been going really great, and I didn't want to mess them up. Or maybe not exactly really great but even, simple, like clean unspooling white string.

After the divorce, I'd wanted someone exactly un-Nathan. Someone who didn't overthink things, who encouraged me to do the same. Doug and I met online in one of those singles chat rooms. Flirting with every large-breasted avatar, he was sardonic and perverted and just a little mean. Our first date, tucked in a large red leather booth in some swanky place he chose in Hollywood, his hand was up my skirt before we were through the smoked ostrich appetizer.

The two of us are not suited to each other in the conventional ways. I work in a suburb outside LA as a guidance counselor at a charter school that emphasizes the connection between art and academics. Though it's not exactly psychotherapy—that boat has sailed—I'm still able to use my degree to help kids. My job is mainly to encourage creativity and assess individual aptitude. Doug, meanwhile, is a divorce lawyer in West LA, cheating the heart-broken soul-weary middle-aged out of their money. Of course, I don't know that for certain. We don't spend much time talking about our respective career paths.

Friday morning, Doug called during recess. He said, *I want to stay in bed all day with you, sip champagne from your belly button, watch dirty movies and use up all the towels.*

By lunch, I'd decided to do it. The idea of getting away from our everyday lives was appealing: my cat that stares morosely at our sex; the nudes in Doug's apartment— lines of disproportionate endowments so crude I know he painted them himself—looking out from the wall with vague, smeared lust.

I liked the idea of myself as someone who would go on a spur-of-the-moment dirty weekend tryst with her lover. I went out on my lunch break and bought an expensive negligee. I tried on about ten before I found the right one: raunchy, hot pink and see-through. When school let out at three, I went to a local salon and had my entire pubic area, except for a thin strip in front, waxed. It hurt like hell, but it's so smooth and soft down there now, like new unformed putty.

⸙

As the sun starts to go down, I put on a white cotton sundress and go for a stroll around the golf course surrounding the property while Doug starts dinner. The afternoon had filled me with a mild sense of dread, the irritation in Doug's voice, the talking hummingbirds.

There are palm trees standing around the green like gawky teenage boys. Also lemon trees, citrus heavy in the twilight. No beaches or large bodies of water, but there are ponds quenching the grass, swallowing the errant white ball, though nobody's out tonight that I can see. The landscape sparkles and shimmers. It has the quality of a place abandoned. Dry heat stretches the sound of my footsteps on the sidewalk.

Nathan, my ex, used to love to golf. He tried to teach me a couple times, but I never took to it. It just always seemed like a big waste of time. So I let him go off without me most weekends, with guys from work or, more frequently near the end of our marriage, with his church group.

Nathan had a spiritual crisis the last year of our five-year marriage. He entered a funk after being fired from his insurance broker job. Usually full of energy and optimism, quick to laugh, he became sad or angry most of the time. He'd do things like sit in front of the television with the sound off and mumble insults at the people on screen.

"Think you're so god-damned special."

"Smile at me one more time, you sonofabitch."

"I'll show you real work."

He lost fifteen pounds. His skin became loose and rough, like fruit left on the windowsill too long. I made him see somebody, a friend from grad school who had a successful practice in the burbs. He got drugs, tried different hobbies, practiced yoga.

Then he started going to church. He found God, which seemed to revive him. He was upbeat and pleasantly beefy, if not around as much. That was OK, as I enjoyed having some quality alone time. I thought it was good we had separate interests, that we could diversify as a couple.

Then one day he told me he couldn't be with someone who doesn't accept Jesus as her lord and savior, and that on top of that, all of the angels had left LA. He was moving to Idaho where a large chunk of them had apparently relocated with a woman from his church named Teresa. He said Teresa had a warm, bright soul that had healed him. It all happened so fast, I don't think I had time to process everything. In my mind, we were perfect for each other. I had such a clear vision of our future—the yard, the children, the turquoise swimming pool on the top level of our biannual Caribbean cruise—that it was almost like it had already happened. After a couple months of numbness, I suddenly hurt terribly. I felt it all over, everywhere in my body at once, a heavy bone ache. I went to Idaho, to their house, and I begged him to come back to me. It was ugly. I screamed and cried and even tried bargaining, telling him I would go to church, that I had always felt a spiritual lack in my life. He remained unmoved.

This other woman, this Teresa, put her arms around me and touched my hair and she was so tender, I put my arms around her back and we held each other like that for a while, until Nathan said I had to leave.

⁘

Walking back to the condo, I make a new resolve to give myself wholly to this fun, sexy weekend.

I stride into the kitchen like a woman with an abundance of sex appeal. There are tomatoes and garlic and lemons and parsley lined up on the counter and Doug is chopping. "Can I help you with anything?" I ask, jumping up on the counter. Doug guts a tomato with the detached swiftness of an executioner.

"No." He points a finger jellied with tomato seeds. "I really like your hair like that."

"Thank you." I clasp my hands in my lap, not sure how these things go. If there's a series of events I should be initiating. I've never been much good at seduction. "All the better to fuck you with."

Doug laughs as he slices the tomato. His strokes are fast and soundless. I feel weird having nothing to do, slightly decadent and empty. Doug's wearing a white linen button-down shirt, unbuttoned, revealing the olive skin of his hairless chest, the few dark hairs from his belly button disappearing in the waist of his slacks. He's the kind of guy I've never had a problem staying away from, the ones wearing tight tank tops at the gym who make vulgar faces with free weights in the mirror, grunting like you know they do during sex.

I reach over and pop a tomato cube in my mouth. He drops the knife and roughly grabs me by the shoulders.

"Let's see it," he says. "You little thief."

We make out on the kitchen counter, slide to the linoleum, pull and crawl our way in front of the fireplace. Dinner is put on hold.

There's something missing, like the light's not quite right, or maybe it's that the carpet is cheap and scratches against my back, digging raw sores along each shoulder blade and at the base of my spine. I feel like if we could just get the right angle, the exact right configuration of limb and lip, this would be perfect.

"I like that humming," he says, lifting my ankle to his shoulder.

Later we drink expensive wine and devour everything Doug's been cooking all day, lobster bisque with endive-mozzarella salad. Slow-roasted veal shank. Doug bakes desserts that are eaten every hour, sugary fruit and soft bits of cake that we scoop up with bare fingers and feed each other. Sex and food: we've broken life down to the basics, the fundamentals. The hummingbirds continue to buzz and whisper at the windows.

Dreams are often most profound when they seem the most crazy.

Neurosis is the inability to tolerate ambiguity.

Sometimes a cigar is just a cigar.

"*The ego is not master in its own house*," I say to Doug, as he lifts a spoon of something steaming and delicious to my mouth.

"What?"

"It means that the id, the subconscious, is what drives us."

"Want to get naked on the counter?"

"We already did it on the counter."

"So?"

·:·

The next afternoon, Doug prepares some kind of small stuffed chicken. Red sauce simmers on the stove and potatoes reeking of garlic and rosemary sit in a bowl.

"See you have to get under it, like this," he says, inserting sprigs of rosemary underneath the chicken skin.

"Do you have to stretch it out first?"

"Gently. Like you were seducing a virgin."

The hummingbirds whisper at the window.

Analogies decide nothing, but they can make one feel more at home.

He takes my fingers, moving them under the skin. It feels disgusting and sexy. I think it must be close to the way it feels to enter a woman.

"Do you love me?" I ask Doug. I know it's the wrong thing to say. I tell myself I don't care what the answer is. But isn't this what we all want, even when we pretend we don't?

Doug kisses my neck and lowers the strap of my sundress. "I think you're very sexy," he says. And I suppose that's a kind of love—an honest love, a physical thing that you can see and feel.

After dinner, Doug stretches out on the couch and falls asleep. I think he probably deserves a little catnap after all that cooking, so I leave him alone while I do the dishes. The pots and knives and cutting boards have piled up in the sink every day, greasy, avalanching sculptures that I must disassemble every evening.

I fill the sink with warm soapy water and immerse my hands for a moment. The water feels like something breathing. Lately it seems like everything is more sensual, everything rubbed swollen. My physical body sloughing off its layers. Every time I move I feel pleasure. Or, more accurately, a throbby heat starting in my core and spreading out until I'm pure vibration.

I think I see a hummingbird in the shadows behind the window, but I can't be sure because everything out there is obscured by my own image. *Being entirely honest with oneself is a good exercise*, they say.

I've given up on my hair, all the rolling around, the knots. Curls jag out from my head like feelers. The reflection in the window fascinates me: a woman who doesn't care. I shake my head for the hummingbird. I say, quietly so as to not wake Doug: *I am wanton.*

After everything is clean, counters wiped down, I go over to the couch and try to wake Doug. I straddle him and kiss his neck. I press my breasts against his chest and rub against his hips. I run my hand up the inner part of his leg, the tip of my tongue along the edge of his ear. Nothing.

-:::-

The next day, the end of our trip, feels like the last few minutes of recess, all the kids scrambling for that one last bit of fun before they have to put the equipment away. When Doug finally joined me in bed the sun was just starting to come up and the room was filled with a sexy half-light and we went at it like teenagers until the room was smothered in sunshine and it was too hot to stay in there anymore.

Doug is now at the store, his second trip today, because he forgot the capers for the bagels, or they weren't the right kind of capers, or he wanted more of a variety of capers. I'm sitting in a lawn chair in my bathing suit on the balcony. The sunlight is clean and warm and my skin melts gradually into the slats of the plastic chair. I look down at my body: skin bloated, stuffed. All the cookies and cakes and rich meats and cheeses feel like they're right at the surface. My bikini line is itchy and covered in red bumps. I never even got to wear the negligee. I close my eyes and try to let it all go: the bloat, the hummingbirds, this heavy ball of something, guilt or sadness or feathers, lodged in my chest.

A hummingbird zips up to the feeder. It takes a couple sips, the dart of its beak barely visible. I move my chair to get a closer look. It's definitely one of the birds that's been hanging around, flashes of red-green iridescence. Though this time I can't make out any words, just buzzing.

The hummingbird lurches at me. Stuck to the chair, I try to duck and cover my face as wings like motor blades scrape my neck, its needle beak stabbing the places between my fingers. My skin sparks like live wire. My legs don't work. My body is a sack of flour. The humming enters me, trilling down my throat, thumping into my chest. Feelings of shame and desire and anger buzz through me, and the hummingbird keeps coming.

When I'm finally able to get up, I open the sliding glass door and run inside. Doug's coming through the front door, and I go to him, sobbing—loud and unpretty. I tell him about the attack in between gulps of air, my fingers trembling as I try to gesticulate correctly. He guides me to the couch and tells me to sit down and take deep breaths.

He walks over to the sliding glass door and looks out. The hummingbird is still there by the feeder, flaunting its ruby throat and teal shimmer, obviously unaffected by our encounter.

Doug turns around and smiles. "Is that the defendant?"

"You don't believe me? You think I made it up? Look at this," I say, tilting my head to expose the attacked side of my neck, pointing to my forehead and cheeks.

"It looks like you've been sitting in the sun and maybe picking at your skin," he says. "You probably fell asleep out there. I'm not saying you're lying: a lucid dream."

"I must have been too close to the feeder or something. You try it, you go out there."

Doug is smirking. He comes to me, puts his hands up my shirt. "I know how to make you forget all about it."

I want to tell him exactly what the attack felt like, the heat pulsing underneath my skin, flit of hummingbird feather like gasoline rainbowing in the sunlight. The flashing, the zagging.

I want to tell him about my soul. It's become loose, unmoored, I have to strap it down before I lose it forever. But his mouth presses hard against my mouth and his hand is down my pants.

I look over his shoulder out the glass door. The

hummingbird is still there and it dips its beak to the feeder. It looks up, silent, suspended in the air, wings a blur of movement. Arcs up and over the roof of the next condo like a firework and then is gone: a pinkish echo against the plain blue sky.

BESTIARY IV: Steller's Jay

The Steller's jay outside your window is not interested in you (don't feel like you have to keep your hands where we can see them.) These birds are mostly found in forests and wilderness areas but are adept at locating backyard bird feeders. Black head topped with a faux-hawk crest, a hipster dipped in peacock blue, shadow half-painted in Technicolor. (Turning down the volume at this point is off the table—don't worry, the neighbors can't hear.) The official bird of British Columbia, Steller's is the only jay west of the Rockies. Inquisitive and clever, the Steller's jay can imitate birds, squirrels, cats, dogs, chickens, and some mechanical objects. (Keep in mind the flesh on the screen is not your own.) These birds are notorious nest-raiders. They are bullies and thieves. But forgiven, as bullies and thieves tend, by their beauty and their flair. The Steller's jay almost allows you to forget your mortality (but your body never lets you forget, does it? Its tingles and itches, the latent ghosts of tumors and infidelities and things scraped off, cut through, scorched.)

Watch the Steller's jay pick apart a worm on top of the moss-covered fence. The way he holds part of it down with his foot, then tears with his beak at the jelly guts (the moans coming from your computer are not your own.) Watch him now take the rest of the worm into his mouth. See the jay's method, merciless and furtive—he knows the god watching him is indulgent only if you pretend your right hand doesn't know what your left is doing.

Apocalypso

The fog might be lighter today. I tell Sonia this, and she smiles. It might, she says, and pours more coffee, that which resembles coffee, as the ocean resembles the ocean—briny expanse, crashing waves. Dirty peach foam, vaguely magenta farther out.

From the terrace we watch the foam suck at the crumbling rock wall. It used to rise to some kind of outdoor stage but is now being slowly consumed by whatever is slowly consuming things here: God, salt, alpha particles. Fog begins the daily routine of melting the gray mountains in the distance, swallows scorched palm trees and thatched umbrellas.

Nobody tells you how boring the apocalypse is. The gray, flat waiting.

Actually, this is the first time Sonia has talked to me in three days, when I heard her searching for a frequency on the CB. I commandeered a walkie-talkie down the hall and intercepted the signal. I thought we could both use a laugh.

"Hello." I dropped my voice an octave. Static sizzled. "Hello, searching for signs of life. Come in, is anyone out there?"

Immediately I was sorry for the excitement in her voice, which has since echoed against her punitive silence while I contemplate whether or not I've ever been able to elicit such a tone, such tremor and hum.

"Hello? Oh my gosh, hello. I'm here. Who is this?"

My first urge was to hang it up—a prank call, wrong

number. But then she spoke again: "Hello? Are you still there? Oh please, please come in." Two walls away I knew the hopeful angle of her chin as she grasped her neck with one hand, reassured herself of the blood still pumping, bright chapped lips parted—a sexual, scientific mouth—breathing all that hope for a person not me.

"It's your loving husband," I responded in my real voice. "I just wanted to know what you'd like for dinner—kidney beans and peas, or refried beans? And we have one more can of pineapple."

Static: bodies at rest, electrical disturbances. What rattles in your chest, alone at the end of the world.

Today, though, all might be forgiven. She hums to the Billy Ocean song playing over the sound system, *sad songs to make you cry*: We are cowards for silence. I close my eyes and over the ocean, under Ocean, the can opener creaks; I imagine slow-roasted veal shanks with mint chutney and creamy mashed potatoes, gobs of garlic and butter. Sonia tells me this only makes it worse, that fantasy will be my undoing, but I believe it good exercise—hope strengthening.

In her former life, Sonia studied rock formations, the aftermath of geological events. She was finishing her post-doc at the University of Colorado when we met at the Grand Canyon. I was a poet trying to make small talk about erosion. We stayed up all night under the bright chaos of stars, and while she spoke of lava flows and the silver iridium scabs left by asteroids, the cracking and pouring and stretching that dictates where and how we live, I tumbled into love.

It's coming, she said. Great stores of carbon in the arctic released. It's already happening. Permafrost isn't so permanent after all.

Yes, but the whales, I said. They're still singing.

Soon the whole ocean will fizz like champagne. Eco-systems change very slowly, until a certain point, and then cataclysm takes over. Like rolling a ball up a hill: right now, we've rolled it to the very top and let it go.

We will destroy ourselves before the earth even has a chance.

It's not an either/or.

When I open my eyes, Sonia is grinning at me over a can of tuna. Actual tuna—the crinkle of brown paper bags. Blue sky and endless chlorine Sundays.

"Where did you—?"

Though it's the middle of the day, Sonia has lit a candle, is pulling the cork through a bottle of wine—one thing we will likely never run out of, the cellar of the old resort packed to the gills with bottles.

I lift my eyebrows. "In the afternoon?"

She pours the wine into two glasses, bright as blood, holds her glass up.

"To us," she says, smiling like the devil.

"What's the special occasion?"

The next and only other CD clicks on, calypso beats that again for a brief moment fool me into thinking we're still on our honeymoon about to drink piña colada out of a pineapple, ask the waiter for more bread.

"I have some news," she says. Those words used to have another connotation, once. She couldn't possibly mean. I study her for flush, but she doesn't look any different. Besides a slight hollow to her clavicle, a few new shadows, she is ravishing, tall and slender as an ibis, her hair now Rapunzel long, kinked with salt.

"And what news is that, my dear?"

"Not yet." She cuts a small piece of pinkish gray fish and puts it in her mouth, closes her eyes with pleasure.

What could it be? I love secrets. There have been so few. Or rather, everything is enshrouded here, little room for manageable mysteries. Even so, sometimes I think this is the best thing that could have happened to us, that we missed a bullet, so to speak, avoided having to live in that other world, the one with corruption and bigotry and cat videos. Though there are few creature comforts here, no creatures whatsoever, it is our world. Every day we wake up survivors, our identity constant as the fog. There is only one thing missing, besides cheese. The thing we don't talk about.

"Scrabble or bridge?" I ask.

"Neither."

"Take a dip later?" I ask.

"You really shouldn't swim in that."

I roll the tuna around in my mouth. Neural firing, windowless rooms full of addicts, starving artists, smug conspiracy theorists: everyone clapping for a bit of canned fish.

She hasn't touched the wine since that first sip. I am paying attention. She glows. A discernible light pulses from within, her eyes clear and bright.

We'll have to be so careful, I think. We had both just assumed it would never be possible, the toxins and radioactive particles and god knows what else floating and swimming and seeping into everything. But life thrives. Given a chance, it beats the odds. I remember once an image on the news of small yellow buds pushing up—sunflowers planted at Chernobyl soaking up the radioisotopes in the soil, both hope and remedy.

I imagine a child running around the pool laughing, carrying out some silly game he invented. We would find a way to clean it. Or fill it with something else—how would he know?—Jell-O. He wouldn't miss hummingbirds or the glittering afterpath of a slug on a sidewalk. Always it will have been magenta waves and ashy fog.

Maybe we'll have more children after that. Repopulate the earth. No wars or disregard for life, filled with an appreciation for the way ash corrupts limestone, the vocabulary with which to sing it. I would take charge. I would do what needed to be done. Fatherhood would cure me of ineptitude and the vice of daydream.

Sonia was pregnant once before. We'd been dating a short time. Sonia's career was just starting to take off; my book was almost finished. I went with her to the appointment, sat beside her as she filled out the forms. The nurse called her name, and she didn't look at me, just let go of my hand and followed the woman beyond the door. While I waited, I did the NYT crossword. It was a Tuesday, so it was still within my capability. I should have been able to finish it in a half hour. But there were several clues that eluded me; I circled like a hawk, hoping to surprise them from different angles, but they remained stubborn, riddles with missing words. I tried not to think about what was happening behind that door, though now the image of Sonia, pale in a white gown staring up at cloud-painted ceiling tiles, is spliced with ten blank squares.

When she came back out, she looked dazed but intact. I didn't know what to say. She was holding a small powder blue plastic bag. I tried to take it from her, but she wouldn't let me. That night, she cried in my arms. I felt sad and protective and, I admit now, also relieved and grateful—wrapping my arms around her, I was able to provide concrete comfort, and it was over. Our lives could go on as they had.

"What's your news?" I take another bite of tuna, a sip of wine. "I'm dying to know."

"Just wait."

"Then dance with me?"

She takes my hand, presses her angles against my angles, hipbones and shoulders moving to a private beat outside the calypso. I wrap my arms around her, vibration beneath her skin. I imagine a life curled within, a small bean. A compact, dazzling seed of energy, unfurling the next Big Bang. I twirl her, the fabric of her dress a loose pale cotton that somehow always looks clean, the outline of her strong body glimpsed through the fabric, and I think: *stay in this moment.*

Then she is behind me, sliding her hands beneath my shirt, and then up to cover my eyes, a game we used to play.

"What were you just seeing?"

I smile, her hands dry and warm on my cheeks. "The most beautiful woman I've ever laid eyes on."

"No. After that. When I moved behind you. What was in front of you?"

"The terrace. Umbrellas. Petrified bird shit."

"You weren't looking." Her hands are sweaty, and I am a little tired of this game. I try to lift her fingers from my eyes, but she presses them tighter.

"Sonia. Enough now."

"Are you ready?"

She lifts her fingers, and the world blinks into existence again: the tables and chairs, the umbrellas, shapes behind the fog. And a bird. Sitting perfectly still atop an umbrella—a seagull, white with light gray wings, bright yellow beak and discerning, scheming beady eyes.

"Can you believe it?" she asks. "I tried to track him yesterday, but he flew over the inlet and I lost him. He can't be the only one, the only life—they're scavengers."

The seagull opens its wings, screeches, and lifts off, disappearing into the fog. Sonia stands in front of me and holds out her hand.

I'm tired. I close my eyes and see seagulls at the shore every summer of my childhood diving for French fries and hamburger buns, cutting their shrill song against the crashing waves. A kiss under a pier, cool sand, saltwater taffy and ketchup. Gardenias on a summer night, bonfire smoke as the night sea sings hamartia and a bottle of cheap whiskey is passed, clothes shed before running into the water, stars in the shape of promises from an honest and generous god, and the waves crash into and around us like gentle bombs.

As a teenager, I used to pick locks. Houses, cars, whatever looked like it might not have an alarm system. It was the give of each pin I was after, that soft click of release. A handful of wood and metal—the barriers are so much more permeable than anyone ever imagined.

Sonia tugs at my hand. There are rooms upon rooms. Pictures on the wall. Knick-knacks, dishes in the sink, shoes in the middle of the floor and always a smell: French toast, sweat, plaster, paint, skin, mold. Sonia tugs at my hand, but I am a rock, a boulder, a wall that will eventually, through no will of my own, crumble into the sea.

BESTIARY V: Chimney Swifts

The swifts group at sunset above the school's chimney: a funnel of flickering birds that disappears down the shaft with the last of the sun—but first they ascend in one flat sheet, loop around trees. The last Audubon count was five thousand. We've learned the swifts are migratory, on their way somewhere warmer, that our chimney is simply a stop along the way. But it's been two months now, and they're still here.

People bring blankets and food, dogs and children. Whatever internal mechanism compels the birds to gather seems to also bring the same people night after night to the same place to watch more or less the same show, as they swoop and swirl down the chimney that no longer functions as a chimney, long ago abandoned for safer heating alternatives.

The bird's simple form, its swept-back wings and cigar body, make it easy to replicate. Swift headbands—two felt birds at the end of antenna springs—are sold at the site, shirts silkscreened with an image of the birds above the chimney, funnel cake, swift koozies and bookmarks and figurines.

Occasionally a falcon or hawk swoops in to grab one of the swifts. People boo, and then, when the swifts move as a unified defensive front to chase away the offender, they clap and holler. Groups emerge. A faction of watchers places bets on whether or not the hawk will appear on a particular night, how many appearances, if it will accomplish its goal, if the birds will chase it, if it will come back a second

time. Some denounce these bets as cruel. Inhumane prof-
iteering. But if anything these condemnations encourage
more to join in. The boos and cheers begin to mix. Fights
break out, usually provoked by biological determinist heck-
ling, devolving into punches and shouted moral precepts.
Do unto the swift. The Audubon workers, ill-equipped in
matters of crowd control, learn to look the other way, and
once the birds have gone into the chimney and the sun has
set, the provocateurs usually lose steam.

Some swear the birds are a sign. Our leaders will become
honest and bold, the earth will heal, break from its blister-
ing crust and shine like polished stone. Others say the birds
are an omen, their shadowy amassing a pantomime of the
devil's. Still others insist the birds are simply nesting along
their migratory route. They warn of reading too much into
it. *Remember the alligators*, they say.

A woman begins to make predictions based on the
pattern of birds, interpreting subtle shifts in the funnel's
shape. The first one is a fire at the southwest edge of town.
Due to a lack of credence, the fire progresses further than
it should have.

For the second, a school shooting, we are better prepared.
A police officer apprehends the student before he even has a
chance to fire. There are a string of other predictions after
that: a suicide, a car crash, a robbery. All averted, thanks
to the woman, and the birds.

It isn't just tragic prophecy; there are marriages, awards,
pregnancies, good weather, ambitious goals successfully
completed. Nobody knows who the woman is or how ex-
actly she does it. The predictions show up, written in blue
ballpoint pen on scraps of old newspaper with the origi-
nal print erased and the week's predictions filled in, every
Monday morning in the school principal's mailbox. Each

one signed with an S. Some people say she's a teacher; otherwise, how would she have access to the building? Mrs. Salesses who teaches third grade and wears costume jewelry. A longtime proponent of papier-mâché and glitter, she's always seemed a little different, in touch with something beyond this world.

How we know the person making these predictions is female is not altogether clear. Something in the language, the slant of handwriting, and the way she puts it down without censor: a fragile, elegant order. Specifics combined with the vague. Mr. Crudner falls off his ladder and breaks his hip. Two people fall in love by the lake. Heavy rain on Tuesday. Incredible sunset Friday. A malignant tumor in someone's right breast. A downed power line on the corner of 4th and Jefferson.

Some of us fall in love with her, our prophetess. Some have elaborate fantasies of her saving us from a burning building, wrapping us in blankets, whispering our own secrets, long forgotten, in our ear.

Not every calamity can be avoided, and interference sometimes has unforeseen consequences. Like the lightning strike, the original target of which was the big oak tree outside the church. In diverting the electricity to a conductor, high voltage transients arc in an unforeseen pattern and end up frying a whole pond of bass. Which leads to a preponderance of bears from a nearby state park, large brown bears that, after gorging on dead fish, start to search through our dumpsters, hang out at picnic areas. Wildlife officials have to find, sedate, and remove them all, though not before Abby, a darling chubby four-year-old lacking a healthy fear of top predators, is snatched from an afternoon game of hide-and-seek. We again recall the alligators.

Some of us still remember that, are old enough to have

actually been there. Fourth of July, the sparkle and bang of fireworks, the lake glittering, patriotic swaying, hot dogs, lovers pulled close. Then all at once screaming, as those we loved and cared for were dragged into the water by the very monsters we'd celebrated, hulking armored lizards risen quietly from the mud.

Afterward, we changed the high-school mascot, the name of the Lucky Gator coffee shop, removed its image from our city crest. We thought we had learned our lesson. We vowed to be more careful, to consider every possible consequence of our actions.

Instead of moving as one unified group, the swifts begin to dart and zigzag as individuals. They still go down the chimney, but before that, it's every bird for himself, a chaos of tangled wings against the molten sky.

What does it mean? We ask each other. Monday isn't for three more days, and we don't know if we can wait. This is big, whatever it is. Maybe S. will make an exception, will give us her prediction early.

So we wait and watch, but the predictions don't come, and the birds continue to perform their confusion. Monday rolls around, and still no newspaper.

One of us claims to see her, not Mrs. Salesses after all, but the girl who works the counter at the Lucky Labrador coffee shop, the one who wears a black ribbon in her hair and makes a perfect heart in the foam of our cappuccino; she was driving out of town, car packed to the roof with belongings. It had to be her—the careful determination with which she gripped the wheel, her mouth forming the words *I'm sorry*.

Some people follow, pack up and leave, not wanting to take their chances.

But some of us still cling to hope. Some of us don't believe S. would just leave like that, right when we need her most. Some of us, steadfast and loyal, stay, watch the chimney, check the mailbox, and wait patiently for our future, even when the sky opens up and the birds begin to drop like stones.

3-D Printing: A Love Story

We printed cups with dust-gray filament. They came out eerily round. When you drank from them, you had to use both hands—not because they were heavy, because they were suspicious.

Next we tried figurines: a basic algorithm for noses and eyes, plastic right angles of hair. Charlie sat the dolls around a table, and I poured them invisible tea from a dull square pot.

Then jewelry and bike helmets and the foam you stab knives into to stop them from cutting.

"What about a car?" Charlie asked. "Take us on the road." I laughed and poured him more invisible tea. But he did it, or something like it: a rectangular bucket, each wheel's diameter the exact difference in our height.

I met Charlie in Introduction to Computer Animation. I was taking it for kicks but Charlie applied himself. He wanted to make films. He wanted to invite the viewer into an immersive experience. The first day he leaned over and, coolly brushing the dreadlocks from his forehead, suggested that for complex polygon faces, I try the paint selection tool. You can use a brush to paint over the faces you want without selecting the obscured ones behind them, he said. I didn't know what he meant exactly, but I knew it was flirting.

We had to make a film in that class. Mine was thirty seconds long: a stick figure falling in love with another stick figure. Stick figure #1 had dropped something on the sidewalk that stick figure #2 picked up, and the something, revealed at the end of the film, turned out to be her heart: bright red, in the shape of a child's valentine. Charlie's film was a 3-D apocalypse adventure, a ten-minute romp through a scorched Grand Canyon. At its center was a ravishing Charlie, rattlesnake for a cohort, battling the demons at the end of the world.

My mother didn't approve of the relationship. She said Charlie was too creative, that I needed someone with both feet on the ground. She never understood progress, how life is an opportunity.

Next Charlie got into confections. He programmed candy snowflakes. Chocolate orbits. We ate until our giddy turned to sick, those perfect shapes dissolved inside us like hot, terrible whispers.

We started to print things we didn't intend. Instruments we didn't know how to play. Tubas with missing tubes, harmonicas without harmony. Stairs that led nowhere. The printer seemed to be reading our dreams. We'd fall asleep to its careful repetitions like a squeaky bed, the smell of melting plastic, and wake to Nixon masks and trick snakes. One morning I found the dog I had as a child, Singapore, curled up half his original size and lime green at my feet.

We couldn't walk around the house anymore. We tried putting some of it out on the lawn, but the neighbors didn't want it either. They sensed something was different. These things were not manufactured through the proper channels. They looked through a blank kaleidoscope, lifted a mute seashell to their ears.

My mother came over and we printed a box for her to get inside. The dimensions were so exact she cried and made me promise to get rid of it.

We began printing containers to put the other things in. At first they were simply functional, just large boxes. Then ones with a door cut into the center, then windows, then pipes. We experimented: perfectly round yurts, rhombus bungalows, and trapezoidal colonials. We filled the street with them, then the city. After housing all our stuff, we opened them up to anyone who wanted to live there.

The homeless vanished. Everyone did, actually. There was more inside than outside, and the printer kept on printing. The printer printed other printers that kept on printing.

Charlie and I went from room to room, not sure anymore which rooms belonged to whom, if they belonged to anyone at all. Each one seemed like the one before but not like any rooms we were used to: rubber and plastic and too many walls. We made up a story for each new room. We were a Hollywood power couple making things happen, a bohemian artist and his muse living off paper apples and peanut butter. Sometimes there were already people in these rooms, and so we incorporated them in our play: *Stick 'em up*, I shouted, pointing a plastic semiautomatic with plastic bullets. Sometimes accidents happened, and we'd have to crawl through basements like bandits.

When I found a dozen plastic pinkies one morning, I looked at Charlie.

"Don't look at me," he said.

Charlie was missing the little finger on his right hand. He was just born that way. He doesn't ever talk about it, but I think it's always bothered him. Sometimes I'll notice him staring at it, at the knob of knuckle that ends in nothing, as if trying to imagine a finger there, or maybe he's thinking something else entirely, about the luck of four-leaf clovers—it's almost impossible to guess what goes through a lover's mind.

"What are we supposed to do with these?" I asked. On further inspection, I wasn't completely sure they were pinkies. It was hard to tell without other fingers to compare them to—or an attached palm—but the plastic looked like real human skin.

"I don't know, but I think we're in trouble," he said.

"Whatever you do," I said, "try not to think. Try to empty your mind."

He was trying, I know he was, I could see the attempt at blankness in his eyes, in the concentrated rise and fall of his chest.

"Kiss me," I said. He opened his mouth and a dozen sailboats, white and perfect, tumbled out like jacks.

"I never knew you dreamed of sailing," I said.

"Neither did I," he replied, though his mouth was now so full of tiny plastic hearts I couldn't be sure those were his exact words.

Summer People

Shasta watched from her kitchen window as the neighbor walked to his car: spiky silver hair, jeans so tight they seemed to give him trouble. He drove an old gray hatchback covered with graffiti. From her vantage point above, it looked like someone's cartoon dream woman had fallen from the window and broken apart and then been absorbed by the crappy matte paint. Across the roof a thick thigh tapered to shapely calf, stiletto heel like something used to slay dragons. Disembodied breasts on the passenger-side door, fleshy globes with dark pointed nipples. They reminded Shasta of her dad's tattoos, the ones that used to mortify her in childhood, that still do—his forearms' twin mermaids, busty pirate pinup on right bicep, cowgirl on his left tangled in her own lasso.

"When's your dad supposed to stop by?" Steven asked, looking over her shoulder, as if reading her mind, which she sometimes thought he could do.

"He said four."

The neighbor drove off, a blur of flesh.

"I met him the other day," Steven said.

"Who?" Shasta removed the cake from the oven while Steven took down liquor bottles. They touched apologetically with minimal eye contact, like airline passengers on the way to the bathroom. Sweat in creases of flesh, windows open with nothing but heat passed in and out.

"The neighbor."

"Why didn't you tell me?" Shasta turned the oven off. It made the whole house unbearably hot, but she couldn't stop baking. Cookies, cakes, muffins. Syrupy berry pies and dense sticky brownies. She thought about sugar all day long and sometimes woke in the night to intense craving, would drag herself out of bed to make chocolate peanut butter cake or lemon meringue, the sifting and measuring bringing calm and order to her mind.

"I didn't think it was important," Steven said.

"Did you ask him?"

"Ask him what?"

"About the noise."

This wasn't, Shasta insisted, noise one was required to ignore in a duplex—loud bass, say, or sex. It was less identifiable, more nuanced. Cranky muffled cries vibrated the walls in bursts during the day and sometimes at night, like an old woman complaining loudly through a paper towel. The kind of thing that could make you crazy by its inexactness.

"I just introduced myself. It seemed an inappropriate time."

"What's an appropriate time, over tea?" she said. "Do you want to send him a formal invitation?" She hated the tone she was starting to use with her new husband, the feeling that she was turning into one of those women who constantly belittle and nag, the ones she encountered all the time at the restaurant, correcting their husbands' orders or snidely commenting on their beverage choices. She swore she would never be one of these women. But something was bubbling up, accumulating, and lately she was starting to question the concept of free will. Maybe this was just what happened. Eventually you couldn't bother to be nice.

"Seems like a cool guy," Steven said. "He works at a museum on the river walk." He cut into an orange and the smell of citrus filled the kitchen. "Maybe you should call him," he said.

"The neighbor?"

"Your dad."

Mack had been stopping by lately, said he wanted to know his new son-in-law, be part of Shasta's life again. The duplex was on his way to work, close to the Whispering Glen trailer park where he'd lived for the last twenty years, ever since Shasta was six years old, where American flags outnumbered plants though the people were nice enough, and Shasta had pleasant early memories of everyone gathered in the summer, dragging their foldout chairs and coolers to the center green space, grilling hot dogs and acting out in gently anarchic ways.

Mack never called first and his visits didn't follow any predictable pattern. Steven thought this was a good opportunity to mend broken bridges, heal some emotional wounds. But Steven didn't have enough experience with bullshit. Mack wasn't interested in being her dad. He wanted something. Exactly what she didn't know, but it wouldn't be anything so insubstantial as love.

The blender hummed to life as she spooned raspberries over the cake. When it stopped, Steven took off the lid and dipped his finger into the bright blue slush.

"So are you going to call him?" he asked.

As she was shaking her head, the doorbell rang. Steven's face lit up.

"Your lips are blue," she said. He quickly rubbed his mouth with the inside of his shirt, revealing new tan and toned abs, as Mack's voice rose from down the hall.

"Damn it's hot in here." Mack filled the room with the smell of smoke and musty towels, a smoldering cigar between his fingers. She tried to wave away a fly. None of the windows had screens, and they came in all day lethargic and greedy. "Where's the sexy car?"

"Just missed it," Steven said.

"Those are some hooters," Mack said.

Steven laughed, and she looked at him. This was what she hated more than anything: Steven didn't really think that was funny, he just wanted Mack to think he thought it was funny. But what if, she thought, he did think it was funny? What if she had no idea who he really was? The other day Steven bought plastic pink flamingo lawn ornaments, a two-pack, and set them up out front. "Leave them," he said. "It shows we have a sense of humor."

Part of her initial attraction to Steven was his pale skin, faint shadows underneath doleful eyes. He used to come into the restaurant where she worked and sit by himself at one of her tables with a newspaper, sigh and shake his head every few minutes. He'd take an hour to eat a bowl of soup, each cold spoonful sipped as if it was his regretful daily duty. There was darkness there, she'd thought. A roiling inner life. He'd done things he wasn't proud of, was haunted by these things. It made him see things more clearly, and that was hard. Things were not meant to be seen clearly. After he finally got up the nerve to ask her out and they'd been on a couple dates, she realized he was like anybody: mostly just bored and disappointed with how life had turned out, stuck in Pueblo at the Lakeview Counseling Center, putting in his time, opening his heart to flirty waitresses with baking disorders.

The darkness she'd sensed turned out to be his patients'. He would tell her their stories, even though he wasn't supposed to. One had been kept in a closet by her mother as a girl, duct tape put over her mouth and eyes whenever she made any kind of noise. Now as an adult, whenever she felt blue, she'd tape herself up. There was another one with PTSD who would go to the pet store whenever he felt an episode coming on, buy half a dozen mice, then take them home and break their little necks one by one. He'd lost two wives that way. Most of the stories were your typical love withheld, emotions manipulated, people dying or trying to die—the world was a sad, sad place.

In bed at night, his breath hot at her neck, Shasta would slip into dreams of vaguely menacing shapes, predators running through wet forests, and would wake refreshed, reborn, as if in sleep her brain repaired itself using other people's pain.

But Steven had taken a leave of absence for the summer, and this new husband— unshaved scruff along his jaw, rested and bronzed—was cheerful and handsome and free of other people's sorrow. She wasn't sure how she felt about this new husband.

"You can't smoke that in here," she said to Mack, who was holding up the half-smoked cigar. He tamped it out in the sink and put it in his shirt pocket.

The three of them sat down on the couch with cake and slushy blue drinks, and she was suddenly embarrassed by this childish combination, then angry with herself for caring. She got up to get another piece of cake.

"So, what, this is like your honeymoon month," Mack said.

"We thought we'd take the summer," Steven said. "It all happened so fast, we just want to enjoy each other for a little bit." He reached over and squeezed her knee.

Mack looked at her and she couldn't tell what exactly his expression was trying to communicate, but she didn't like it.

"Her mom and me got married quick, too."

Shasta hadn't told Steven much about her mother. That she left. That Mack was kind of a dick about it. That it was hard, but then life is. He'd tried asking follow-up questions but Shasta told him the truth—she didn't remember her, barely at all. She left when Shasta was five, but maybe she wasn't really there before that either, because the only thing that came was a vague image of her lying on the lawn in her bikini, Mack pressing a cold beer to her back, her screaming at him to knock-it-the-fuck-off.

"Love at first sight?" Steven said.

"She was pregnant." Mack picked off the fruit skewer balanced on his drink and dropped it on the coffee table.

Rain whispered outside the open windows, casting the room in shadow, coating the lawn's pale grass. Not long or heavy enough to penetrate the dry cracked earth beneath, but enough to cool the air a bit. Thunderstorm season. Her favorite part of Colorado summers were those quiet gray afternoon clouds full of electricity. You could smell them, chalk and watermelon: a brief erratic joy.

"Tell me what you think of that," Steven said. "It's something I invented. I call it a Famous Blue Raincoat. I'd love your professional opinion."

Mack brought it to his lips hesitantly. Shasta had to hand it to him: he was trying, in his own way. He took a sip and raised his eyebrows.

"That's really something."

"I found this book—*The Bartender's Bible*—in a kitchen drawer when we moved in. I've been experimenting. You like it?"

"It's very refreshing."

Shasta shoved cake in her mouth. It was a cream of coconut cake with cream cheese frosting. Sour cream and cream of coconut kept it moist, and the flaked coconut on top got lightly toasted in the baking process, offering a slight sweet crunch.

"What's that sound?" Mack asked.

They all sat quietly and listened. There was the regular trill through the wall, then the lower *wha-wha-wha*.

"Cats, I think," she said.

"Sounds kinky," Mack said.

They were in the duplex to save a little money while looking for a house. The idea was to take time and relax before starting the official rest of their lives. But the novelty of not working, able to bask in their new romantic union, spend all day in bed, feed each other ice cream in the bathtub, had begun to wear off. Shasta had retired from waiting tables, was casually looking at community college. Instead of opening, time had begun to behave differently. Accordion minutes, days both infinitely long—so there was always *later*—and abrupt. Only when she awoke in the night did she realize another had passed.

She got on the computer in the living room at two in the morning, vanilla butter cream cake in the oven, and looked at houses with listings out of their price range, imagined life with three floors and a pool. She skipped the ones Steven tagged: single-level town homes with concrete patios. They had twenty thousand dollars saved, half of which was given to them by Steven's parents as a wedding gift. It was enough for the down payment on a single-level town home. Which was perfectly suited to their present situation, more than she'd ever owned. So how to explain this need, a longing almost sexual, for butler's pantries and hand-scraped wood floors, outdoor living rooms and three-car garages and fireplaces—direct-vent, a ribbon of flame writhing behind embedded glass—in the bathroom?

The computer pinged. Mack. His new thing: surprising her in the virtual world same as the real one.

Can't sleep?

No.

Remember when I used to read 2 u when u couldn't sleep?

No.

When u were little

Never happened.

U were once a little girl. Sweet + kind + cute.

I'm busy.

I used to read u those myths.

That book was so racist.

What are you talking about? U loved that book.

Gotta go.

Another big day doin nothin tomorrow?

Goodnight.

Sweet dreams, baby girl.

"Pueblo was founded on a massacre," Steven read. "As part of a larger Colorado raid, the Ute murdered fifty-four Northern New Mexican and Anglo settlers of El Pueblo on the Arkansas River."

They sat in lawn chairs out front of the duplex. Shasta wore a bikini, even though she knew she didn't have the body for it, especially now, with the extra summer-baking pounds. But the slight breeze felt good on her bare skin, sun like marinade. The plastic slats of the chair glued her in place, so that she had to feel around on the ground for her melted strawberry daiquiri. Steven was reading from a book called *Hiking Through Colorado History*. It had a cartoon of a dorky guy with a knapsack and a walking stick on the front cover.

Two small boys walked past wearing heavy baggy clothes, jeans sagged almost to their knees. One of them, a gold chain around his skinny neck, looked at her and then whispered something to his friend that they both thought was the funniest thing they'd ever heard.

"The flood of 1921 wiped out hundreds, diverting the river a half-mile to the south where it stayed. The poorest lived on low ground by the railroad. When the levees crumbled, they were washed away, their bodies floating alongside the bloated corpses of horses. Then the silver mines—explosion, collapse, carbon monoxide poisoning—the names of the dead lost forever."

"Pueblo is a bummer," she said.

"You should know this stuff," Steven said. "It's part of your narrative."

"What narrative?"

"Mack said your great grandfather was an Ute warrior."

Shasta rolled her eyes.

"People say you can still see them," Steven read, "these settlers and miners, wandering the new river walk under a full moon, perplexed by all the concrete, pulling up nasturtiums."

Shasta told him how when she was in high school, the thing to do on a Friday night would be drive out to the old Freely place on the east side of town, what used to be the bad side. In 1975, Mr. Freely lost it and shot his dog. When his wife found out, he shot her, too, then their son. His five-year-old daughter he hung from a rope in the front yard. If you stayed quiet and turned your headlights off you could still see her, made of starlight and tree bark and heartache, swinging from the branches of the oak out front. The house itself had burned down in the 80s, and nobody had done anything with it until a couple years ago when money started moving into the neighborhood and it was torn down, oak tree and all, to make way for a big white colonial with a wraparound porch. One time her date for the evening got so spooked that he broke the rules: turned on the headlights and then sped out of there, tires screeching. As he drove off, she glanced in the rearview mirror and there she was, the girl, glowing with twigs sprouted from her head like antlers, who looked at her, wide sorrowful eyes that accused her of something. But when Shasta looked again, there was just an empty backseat.

"It was probably your own reflection," he said.

She sucked on her straw until it slurped. Steven immediately took the glass from her and went inside.

This was love, she thought: refills without having to ask.

Shasta held the plate out to the neighbor, and he put his hands in the pockets of his robe. He looked annoyed and also, maybe, a little guilty?

"I was making cookies, and I heard you," she said.

"Sorry if we were keeping you up," he said. "Norma and Harold over there," he gestured to a cage in the corner taking up half his living room. "They're in the middle of a lover's spat." He stepped back, not enough to invite her in but enough to reveal two birds in the cage, big colorful parrots. Blue wings, yellow necks, black hooked beaks. Dark lines expanded in webs around their eyes like drawn-on wrinkles. Their names fit them—an old married couple. They began to squawk and move around, crawling up the sides of the cage using coordinated, agitated movements of their beaks and talons. There was the smell she'd been getting whiffs of, but stronger now: sawdust and lettuce rot.

Shasta never had a pet when she was younger. It didn't make a lot of sense to her. That you would keep a live thing in a cage, locked up in a house, for your own pleasure. It seemed cruel and selfish. Especially birds. The whole point of birds was flight.

The only time she got close to having a pet was after one of her and Mack's fights. He'd disappeared for two days without a word, and Shasta was prepared to hate him forever. But she walked in after school, and there he was drinking a beer on the couch like nothing happened. There was a box on the other side of the couch with holes gouged in the top of it.

"What is this?" she'd asked.

He held up his right arm, the blond mermaid covered in scratches. "She's a feisty one."

Shasta tore off the tape, opened the box, and out jumped one of the feral cats that lived by the dumpster behind the Methodist church. The week before she'd seen this one tearing the entrails from a snake, twitching its head as it tried to get through the snake's tougher parts, a glazed look in its eyes. It looked like a small tiger, part of its right ear chewed off.

"Why is she in our living room?"

The cat slinked under the couch, and Mack grinned and bent his head, as if to say: I'm sorry.

The cat didn't last the week. After days of coaxing and rewards, Dragon finally relented to some civilized petting, then took off the second the front door opened. Shasta spent weeks trying to lure her back, bringing bacon and tuna to the dumpster. Dragon would take the food and let Shasta touch her raggedy fur, but the second she reached out to pick up the cat, she'd run away. Eventually the church closed down and the cats found some other place to haunt. Shasta kept on feeding the crows for a while, until Mack asked her where all the bacon was going.

"They're not really used to visitors," the neighbor said now.

"How long have you had them?"

"Almost ten years." He remained in the doorway, neither taking the cookies from her nor asking her in. She wondered if he had something in there he didn't want her to see. "They were my wife's."

"Did she pass away?"

"Five years ago." He was older than she thought, mid-forties she guessed. His hair was gray, but his skin still looked young. Eyes with the same type of alert intelligence as his birds. He was wearing a ratty checkered robe over jeans and moved his wrists around in his sleeves as if to keep warm, even though it was sweltering. She was still holding the plate of cookies, suddenly heavy and silly in her hands, such an obvious trespass at this time of night.

"I'm sorry for your loss," she said.

"Thank you."

"Where did you meet her?"

His annoyance was growing. She felt his gaze before he responded, aware of her lived-in tank top, braless nipples probably showing through the thin fabric. Hair stringy from the heat, hanging in her face. People sometimes said she was pretty but didn't know it. Men said this. They thought it was a compliment, but it wasn't. She kept her eyes on the birds—they were still watching her with a fidgety vigilance but had stopped climbing.

"At the zoo. She was a bird trainer, and I was painting a mural on the wall beside the falcons. She talked to them like they were family members with drinking problems."

One of the birds commenced a low humming, and then the other bird took it up.

"That's a new one. Something they've learned from

you, I believe."

It was the sound, she realized, of Steven's blender. She laughed.

"I'm Shasta," she said. She could see unframed canvases lining his living room wall, swirls and dashes and clouds of bright color—exotically feathered hurricanes, furious rainbow-spitting skies. They clashed with the shabby thrift store couch but matched the birds perfectly. They looked too expensive for someone who drove an old car covered in pornographic graffiti.

"Like the mountain, or the cola?"

"Both, I guess."

One of the birds said, "What the fuck."

Shasta looked at the neighbor, and the bird said it again, this time vehemently, spitting the "fuck" like a pissed-off old man.

"Something my wife taught him." The neighbor smiled, or tried to smile but didn't feel quite up to the task.

He finally took the plate from her.

"Thanks for the cookies, Shasta."

She nodded. He nodded. His hand was on the doorknob now, and he was inching it closed.

"My father named me after a bar he used to work at," she said, and stepped back. "He's a bartender."

"Well, it suits you," he said, and closed the door.

A priest walks into a village—or is it a marketplace?—and turns his walking stick into four eggs, two a vibrant blue, two brown, and tells the people that one set of eggs will turn into brightly-colored birds that will bring an endless summer to their lands, fertility to their crops, and the others will bring a perpetual winter. The first eggs, a bright enchanting blue, the blue of blood under living skin and clear skies, are grabbed first. But these hatchlings grow to be an inky black and take off cackling, bringing upon the people and their crops a perpetual winter: the raven. Those left with the plain brown eggs watch as their birds become the macaw, large beautiful birds in colors of grass and fruit, bringing them forever summer. The Winter People are stronger, having to work harder at tilling their land, but their lives are cold and bitter. The Summer People are soft, carefree, happy.

This was one of the stories from the book of myths, their favorite. When she couldn't sleep, Mack would sit in a chair beside the pullout and read to her, even though she had every word memorized. Then she didn't mind the sour alcohol breath, ice in his glass jingling in the story's pauses. Though the entire book was a simplistic and offensive appropriation of a rich and varied culture, she was unaware of this then; she loved the sweeping animal drama and the pictures: outspread rainbow wings, slinking coyotes, buffaloes up on hind legs.

The reading started after her mom left. Shasta didn't remember the actual leaving, only the not coming back. How one morning it was just the two of them. Mack fried up a couple eggs and poured some milk in a glass and said that certain people had a hard time acting like regular human beings, and her mother fell into this category. And that was the last time they talked about it. Whenever Shasta tried to bring her up after that, Mack turned quietly inward.

"Those Winter People really got the shaft," Mack would say after finishing the story.

"No they didn't. They're strong—look at them, they're bigger."

"That's true." Even then he had a beard, though it didn't have the gray in it yet, and he'd flick the sides as he talked like an on-off switch. "But they were fastest, they knew what they wanted and reacted quickly. They should have been rewarded, not punished, for their initiative. Those Summer People were just slow and lazy, got everything handed to them."

All Shasta knew as a child was she wanted those birds, the blues and yellows so bright they made her mouth water. "So maybe we should be slow and lazy."

"No. You work hard. And then make sure to get your fair share."

⁘

"Tell me about that girl again," Shasta said. They were in bed on top of the sheets, the fan blowing warm air over them. With the windows glued shut, it was difficult to keep the air moving. Duct tape zigzagged like lightning across one of the panes. The sun had gone down hours ago but the sky outside the window was still bright with a full moon and streetlights and the bleary residue of heat.

"What girl?" Steven asked. He had been almost asleep, she could tell by the way he slurred his words.

"The girl with the tape."

"What about her?"

"Just tell me the story again."

"Shasta, I'm tired. Why don't you just go to sleep."

"I can't sleep."

The fan ticked after each turn. Steven's back was to her— his skin had started to peel so that the tan parts looked like dirt. She reached out and peeled off one long strip, then let it drift down to the carpet.

"What did you say to Mack?" she asked.

"When?"

"When I was in the bathroom?"

"I didn't say anything. I don't know. We talked about

the bar."

"Just be careful what you tell him. Don't give him any information. Like about us, about our plans. Please."

"Shasta, I think you should give him a break. He's trying."

The birds next door began their incantations.

"She once said," Steven started, as if remembering something funny, "that she knows the combination to a safe in an underground crypt in Egypt."

"What does that mean?"

"I have no idea. She insisted—she told me to write it down, the number. Who knows, maybe she's right."

"That's not how the story goes," she said.

"What story?"

A woman's scream woke her. Her heart pounded. Through the wall, there was more yelling, both a man's and a woman's voice, and then a crash.

"Hey." She shook Steven's shoulder. "Listen."

He lifted his head and mumbled like someone drugged.

"Fighting. It sounds like a woman being hurt."

"Who's fighting?"

"The neighbor."

His eyes slit open, but by then it was quiet, just the low familiar vibration of the birds.

"It's just the birds," he said.

"No. A woman screamed."

"Do you want me to call the police?"

She had never called the police on anyone. It was an unspoken rule: you took care of your own business. If there was a problem, you handled it yourself.

"You go over there."

"Okay," Steven said. "One minute." He lay on his back and closed his eyes, and within a minute he was snoring.

The neighbor's door slammed, and Shasta got up and went to the window. A woman with long dark hair staggered onto the lawn. Shasta couldn't see her face. She moved in the streetlight like someone drunk. The neighbor came out and grabbed her arm, said something stern that Shasta couldn't hear.

They stayed talking on the lawn for a couple minutes, and then finally the woman followed him back inside.

She could be his captive, Shasta thought. That happened, Stockholm syndrome, or maybe she felt so threatened she couldn't leave. Shasta had read about the fever loop of abuse, the intoxicating push-pull of violence and apology. Like the girl with the tape over her eyes and mouth—sometimes it became the only thing you knew.

She got back into bed but remained alert. Eventually she must have fallen asleep, because the next thing she knew it was almost noon and the room was a hundred degrees and Steven had left a note on the fridge saying he was gone to the library.

This bar was different than his previous place of employment, though just as seedy. How Mack liked them, dark and filled with the smell of piss and smoke, a layer of stink over everything: no wiping down or mopping required. Colored lights hung over the bar in haphazard loops, large plastic shark on the wall with Mardi Gras beads dangling from its tail. Near the door sat a vat of peanuts, and their shells crunched under her shoes. She pretended to hate it, avoided bars in general but especially this variety, what other people accurately called hole-in-the-wall: a gaping black hole that prevented anything from escaping. But there was also something comforting, a feeling of acceptance and belonging—black holes sucked up everything without judgment.

"Isn't this a pleasant surprise," Mack said.

She took a seat at the bar. "Jack on the rocks."

"That's my girl."

The ice crackled as he poured the whiskey. When she was young, after her mom left, she hung out at Shasta's the bar a couple times a week after school when there wasn't anyone to watch her. Mack worked mostly day shifts then, and he would make her Shirley Temples the color of rubies with loads of maraschino cherries, give her a handful of quarters for the jukebox, and tell her not to bother him. Mack said children can be seen but shouldn't be heard—though occasionally he would ask for her opinion. What did she think, should her old man get another tattoo? Was Nancy prettier than Sherry? How young is too young?

"And what brings you in this evening?" Mack asked her now.

"I just wanted to say hi. See where you work." This was only partly true. She'd had a vague idea when she left the apartment of asking him to help her figure out what was going on next door, maybe confront the neighbor, send him a message that there are people keeping an eye on him, backed by Mack's unapologetic blunt presence. But now that she was here, with the sad smell of old beer, she wasn't sure what she wanted.

"And I thought you were avoiding me."

There were two other guys sitting at the bar. One of them, black bomber jacket, raw-looking skin with deep pocks, stared at her with no pretense of doing something else.

"How is the boy?" Mack asked, as if referring to someone's child he didn't know very well. "He's a hoot."

"Oh, yeah? How so?"

"Oh, I don't know." A silent exchange with the other patron, and Mack grabbed a bottle from the cooler, popped off the cap, and swapped it for the empty. "So sincere."

"Some people think that's a good thing."

"Do you?"

She reached over and grabbed a plastic sword from a cup by the napkins. She used to have a whole collection. Other girls played with Barbie while she staged elaborate battles between sword-wielding cocktail monkeys.

"Cats next door still bugging you?"

"Turns out they're birds. You get used to it." She drank what was left in the glass, savored the warmth spreading from her solar plexus to her chest. "But I think something fishy's going on over there. There was a fight last night."

"What kind of birds?" the guy who'd been staring at her slurred. She was surprised she still had the ability to translate.

"Macaws," she answered him.

"Like the story," Mack shouted and grinned. It was like his entire foray into fatherhood had been vindicated.

"Yes, like the story."

"A domestic dispute?" Mack asked.

"I guess," she said. "A woman screamed. It woke me up. Then I saw him grab her arm outside and drag her back into the house."

"What're macaws?" the guy asked.

"Leave the girl alone, Carl." Mack used the voice he always used with his regulars, gruff affection, like a stern babysitter. "She doesn't want to talk to you."

"They're like parrots," she said to the regular. "Anyway, Steven thinks I'm being paranoid. I was hoping you might help me or something."

"Do they talk?" the regular asked.

"Yeah, they do," she said, looking at Mack.

"What do you want me to do? Go over there, rough him up?"

"Maybe just talk to him."

"You know that really isn't my thing, baby girl."

"What do they say?" the regular asked.

Mack winked at her. "Hey, while I've got you here, I wanted to ask your advice about something." He flicked the sides of his beard and looked into the distance while she waited for him to continue. "They're closing the bar."

"What bar," the regular asked, something almost lucid registering in his pale blue eyes. "This bar?" He looked around him like he'd never seen the place before, like he just woke up there by some strange accident.

"That's too bad," she said. "Why?"

"I guess the owner's selling to a guy who plans to turn it into some kind of health food smoothie restaurant."

"Did this guy offer you a job?" she asked. She tried to imagine Mack juicing wheatgrass, growing his hair long, espousing the benefits of ground flax seed and bee pollen.

"No. Haven't been able to find anything. It seems the market for an aging bartender in this town has dried up."

"So what are you saying, you're moving?"

"I'm thinking about it. Friend of mine's got a ranch in Montana. He needs some help. Little stuff, general maintenance, said he could give me work, and room and board."

"I think you should go," she said. "It might be fun. Fresh air, get your cowboy on." She forgot how much she liked this, sitting at the bar and having his full attention. No matter how many times she decided to write him off, this feeling remained, this thrill.

"Maybe I'll learn to ride a horse."

She nodded. "I could see that."

He looked suddenly uncomfortable, shifting back on his heels, lips pressed together. He grabbed a rag and started to wipe down the bar.

"How long would you do that for?" she asked.

"I don't know. A little while, I guess." He shrugged. "I was hoping you might lend me a few dollars." He put a new beer in front of the blissed-out regular.

Her chest constricted. She thought about the inside of his skin, his tender organs, everything dark and throbbing.

"We really don't have any money right now." She drank the last of the watered-down whiskey in her glass.

"That's not what I heard." He looked at her then, lifting his eyebrows as if she were in on the joke.

"I don't know what Steven told you, but we need that money. We're buying a house." The blood rushed to her face.

"Shasta, I know you're still mad at me, and I don't blame you."

Three young people walked into the bar. Two guys and a girl, loud and caught up in a private joke, in the funny fact a bar like this still exists, the embarrassing irony of Mardi Gras beads. One of the guys grabbed a handful of peanuts and started pelting his friend.

"I wasn't a very good father. I was drinking a lot," he said. "I'm done with all that stuff."

The girl walked up to the bar. "Does the jukebox work?" she asked. She was thin and pale with wild red hair, a sex appeal that fluttered and drifted like leaves.

"Takes quarters," Mack said. "What can I get you to drink, darlin'?"

"Can you do a blue malidew?"

"I'll mix you up something special. If you don't like it, it's on me."

Mack produced a frothy pink drink, and the girl took it and joined the boys at the jukebox. They passed it around and the music started, an old poppy sentimental song. Their limbs entwined, snaking and curving through the air as if they were underwater.

She watched Mack wipe down the bar, rinsing glasses in the sink, refilling the plastic swords and straws, able for the first time to really study him, the new lines and sag his face had acquired, additional broken capillaries around his nose. It was a strange and dangerous thing, she thought, the stories people shared.

One of the boys lifted the girl into the air, her laughter shaking down on them like broken glass, and the regular to her right snorted and cracked open a peanut.

"Polly want a cracker?" he asked.

The neighbor was shuffling through his trunk. She'd been watching him from the window and now was outside on the street barefoot, shifting her weight to keep the pavement from burning her feet, not remembering exactly how she got from there to here.

"Hey," he said. "Shasta."

She realized he'd never told her his name.

"Hi," she said. "Going somewhere?"

"Just heading to the store. I'm out of ice."

This sounded like a lie.

"It's pretty easy to make," she said. "It's really just water."

She could hear Mack's motorcycle. He said he was going to stop by on his way to work, but she'd hoped he wouldn't get there before Steven got back from the store. She didn't feel equipped to deal with him by herself, especially after he'd asked her for money.

"I like a lot of ice," the neighbor said.

"I saw you the other night," she said. "With that woman."

He looked amused. "Oh yeah?"

"Who is she?"

"I'm sorry, Shasta, but I don't think that's any of your business."

"I heard shouting. I saw you grab her arm. I should have called the police."

"You go ahead and do that." Was that a threat?

"Why do you have pornographic images on your car? Don't you think that's a little offensive?"

He shrugged. "My friends did it," he said.

"Why?"

"To cheer me up I guess."

"After your wife died?"

He shrugged again, then got into his car and started it up. He drove off, hand out the window in a noncommittal wave. She waited there for a while, but Mack's bike never materialized.

The neighbor's door was unlocked. She called out first to see if anybody was there, then closed the door behind her and moved deeper inside. It was dark, cool, the curtains drawn. The layout was exactly the same as their place, except everything usually on her right was on her left. The birds were sitting in their cage. They stared at her.

One of the birds, she decided it was Harold, moved his head in a side nod, like how a teenage boy would get his bangs off his face or someone would signal the swat team to move in. He rolled his black tongue around between the sharp hooks of his beak. The other one lifted her leg and held up her talons, opening and closing them in some kind of code.

The neighbor's bathroom was surprisingly pleasant with nice-smelling individually wrapped seashell soaps in a basket on the back of the toilet. Down the hall, the bedroom was also clean and vacant of women tied up and gagged. The bed made. A framed picture on the dresser of the neighbor

and a girl with long black hair—the one from the lawn—
smiling on a pier, a seagull posed like a president in the
background. The bedroom closet was organized and un-
cluttered, a few things on hangers, shoes stacked neatly on
the floor. She felt a vague disappointment.

She went back to the living room. In the cage, the other
bird, Norma, cocked her head. Shasta stared into her eyes.
The bird blinked, and her eye seemed to flash, like whatever
she saw in that darkness was a revelation almost immedi-
ately forgotten. She continued to stare, and Norma stared
back, and Shasta felt they were sharing something import-
ant: an exchange of female solidarity. Shasta unhooked the
latch and opened the cage. After some coaxing, both birds
wobbled out.

It felt good, like she was doing something good, freeing
these birds, though the birds themselves seemed unfazed.
At first they just walked around the living room ignoring
her. But then a minute later, Harold became agitated. The
bird flapped his wings at the rocking chair in the corner
that he had somehow set to rocking. "What the fuck," the
bird cried. "What the fuck."

She clucked her tongue and tried to get Harold to calm
down. "It's okay," she said. Norma was in the corner qui-
etly working on some twine. Shasta called to her. She ap-
proached the bird with the idea of picking her up, but Norma
flapped her wings and flew onto the back of the couch and
started screeching.

Once outside, she decided, they would calm down. And
sure enough, as soon as Shasta opened the door, Harold
bolted onto the lawn. But then he just sort of ran around
on the grass in a crazed, slightly hobbled way, and she be-
gan to realize he couldn't actually fly. What would he do
for food? What about the heat? And someone would surely

just snatch him and put him in another cage. She tried to catch him but every time she got close, he would take off. She looked around for help, but there wasn't anyone outside. She felt the neighbors watching from their windows.

"What the fuck," she shouted to them.

She went back into the duplex, thinking she might lure Harold in with Norma. The door open, she beckoned. Norma paced, obviously the smart one, aware of the dangers outside. Harold continued to lurk the periphery of the lawn.

Finally she gave up and crouched by the window. After a minute, Norma came over and looked out with her. They both watched Harold through the window as he tottered off across the grass, wings flapping. He paced for a while like that, like an old man trying to make a decision.

Steven pulled up then and got out of the car. He lifted a bag of groceries from the backseat. Harold, still on the lawn, took one look at him and began to run-flap in the other direction. Steven stopped short, then looked up and saw her in the neighbor's window. She waved and he squinted his eyes. Then they all watched as Harold took the long way around one of the flamingos, and then he was around the corner, and he was gone.

BESTIARY VI: One Hamster

Things were getting out of hand. You couldn't go a dozen steps out your front door before encountering a dog, usually two or three—all straining in different directions, the owner a frazzled puppet with too many strings. Without introduction, one of these canines might press a wet nose against your knee, sniff your crotch, or at the last minute pretend you don't exist, tramp through the mud at your feet as you stumble and apologize (to whom, exactly?). It was no longer safe to roll around in our own front yards. You couldn't hear yourself think over the incessant barking.

A majority vote. Each resident was allowed one dog and owners had three months to find new homes for their extra dogs. Some left them with family members in other towns, or took out ads. A few drove out to the neighboring nature preserve to let their extras loose. Better to be free, the reasoning went, than imprisoned in a shelter. Some families left, decided they didn't want to live in a town that would make such a rule. Which was fine because the ones left were self-selected, were on board.

Many who were initially a little resistant admitted the advantages: it was a whole lot more peaceful, for one. Owners hadn't even realized what a juggling act it had been. Our picnics and barbecues were more civilized. Fewer ankle-twisting divots, no disappearing sausages. The remaining dogs were better groomed, well-behaved.

If we'd stopped there, everything would have been just fine. But some people insisted we take it further. If it worked for the dogs, why not try other pets as well? One fish, one cat, one bunny, one iguana. Then more simplification: one car, one winter coat. We stopped short of one child, because we all knew how that one would go. But one romantic partner did make the books, which upset a lot of people.

There were tunnels dug in the twenties, bootlegger passages that used to connect a few of our most respected establishments, once clandestine speakeasies. The tunnels had gone unused for decades. Nobody was confident in their structural integrity. But rumors started after the initial legislation was drafted: People had cleaned them out and placed rugs and lanterns, tables and benches. Food carts and microbreweries popped up. It was told you could rent a bike down there, or ride a zip line from beginning to end, buy cheap electronics. Underground was supposed to have the best jazz, the raunchiest burlesque, gourmet shish kebabs.

Most of us wouldn't go down there out of principle; we had worked hard to make this town, the above-ground one, a special place. The rules were there for a reason.

Though our teenagers felt differently. Rarely did a season go by without some kid disappearing. They were never gone very long but would reemerge changed. Critical, malcontent. For every answer, they had another question. *Why can't I have more than one tattoo? Why are all the paintings in the house watercolor seascapes? What did you do with Sniffles?*

Another meeting was called, another vote cast, and it was decided that those who had gone down would not be allowed back up. We developed a system for identifying the defectors, a list maintained by a respected set of rotating gatekeepers. Once on the list, it was almost impossible to rejoin the community.

We couldn't actually bar anyone from living here, but we could make it difficult. We used the cold shoulder and the right to refuse service. Heckling and derision. Those under eighteen could be rehabilitated at a special center opened for that very purpose. They were impressionable; they knew not what they did. As for the rest: their choice revealed a lack of faith, misplaced loyalty.

There was a difficult transitional period, in which underground housing areas were constructed, and people said their goodbyes to lovers and family members.

But once we made it through that, just like with the dogs, things got easier. There was more everyday satisfaction. Crime was almost nonexistent. We more firmly embraced our neighbors and grocery store bag boys. Those who stayed had chosen to remain a part of the community, declined the promise of dark thrills, of exotic food and sexual freedom, for what we offered: safety, simplicity, comfort.

Who saw it coming, that fuzzy cloud traveling at breakneck speed over the hills east of the nature preserve?

The extra dogs had somehow formed a pack, had completely thrown off their domestication and were looking for blood. Luckily we got the word out in time to save almost everyone. There were only two casualties above ground— one police officer, one small child—before we were able to sound the alert. Unfortunately, those underground were unable to hear our warning, and the pack demolished one entire tunnel. It took us weeks to remove the bodies, clean out the space and board up the entrance.

Nobody has been able to catch the dogs yet, but we developed a system of bells and horns to indicate where the pack is at any given time of day. We remain mostly indoors now anyway, just to be safe. But there is a certain kind of freedom in that, permission to withdraw and cherish, nurture the private soul.

As the kids say: one hamster one love.

Adventures in Wildlife

Nina thought there was something a little off about the coyotes. Huddled by the lagoon, in high grass between paper mountains and plastic tundra, some struck the usual poses of affable curiosity, nosing the air, pawing the ground. Others seemed different, haunches angled for movement, black lips about to curl. After the ride's first turn, these others appeared closer, so close she could smell them. A combination of hot plastic, moss, musty sheets, and, maybe, blood? Something vaguely nostalgic and embarrassing, like the smell of herself, what still has the power to surprise her, detected on the sleeve of a sweater that's been sitting in her hamper, what she's always afraid has lingered when another girl goes into the bathroom stall at school after her.

She couldn't remember exactly what they looked like before, but there seemed a new flicker and shimmer to their coats. A precision, a desire to live around the ears.

Nina tried to communicate this to the boy next to her, but Jay had been with Nina on this ride five times now and she had yet to so much as touch his zipper. He put his tongue in her mouth to invite silence then tried to coax her hand, which she intended to keep in her lap, and so there resulted a static tug of war, his hand on top of hers, their cross purposes accumulating force like the start of a universe.

After the first turn on the tracks, as they moved deeper into darkness and the air became thick and warm, Karissa pressed herself against the side of the car, crossed her legs. She didn't want to give Devin the wrong idea. Any idea. In the car in front of them, Nina was making out with Jay. From this angle, they were a strange bird creature: Jay's fuzzy buzz cut the face, Nina's sharp chin the beak.

Jarrod had been smoking by the Elephant Swing when they first got there. Haloed by light. Wearing those jeans Karissa loved, frayed at the edges and so dark blue they were like the deepest part of the night. He'd caught her eye, both had nodded in mutual admiration. But, loyal and steadfast to the end, Karissa had forsaken her own thrill and followed Nina to her rendezvous with Jay, and so now instead of Jarrod's fingers in her hair, she had to pretend interest in the animatronic Grizzly (had its eyes always had that shine to them?).

Honestly Karissa probably would have let Devin if he tried; she thought he was kind of cute with his red Converse and dopey eyes. Not as cute as Jarrod but still. Maybe over the bra. Except Devin didn't possess the confidence. His jeans were too light, baggy but not baggy enough, that in-between space that signaled a lack of intuition, any natural knowledge of fashion. And you could tell he knew this about himself, that he didn't even have the ability to pick out an appropriate pair of jeans.

They'd been on this ride before. Nina and Karissa had grown up at this amusement park, a cheap knockoff of Disneyland with a wildlife theme, the park's mascot an anatomically doubtful raccoon, floppy beagle ears, lopped-off rabbit tail. Reilly the Raccoon and his friends—Choco the Cheetah, Wally the Walrus, Katy Kangaroo—liked to sneak up on unsuspecting children and scare the crap out of them. Both had early memories of just such a scare, a scar they agreed probably changed their attitude toward real animal encounters forever after.

They'd grown out of the amusement park for all genuine purposes, with its cutesy creatures and slow kiddie rides, but it maintained an ironic charm. And it was the only place in town where they could escape the watchful gaze of parents and neighbors, especially in the semiprivate dark of Adventures in Wildlife, where, after the sun has gone down and all the kids have gone home but the ride—inexplicably—continues, anything goes, where the digitally manipulated bird calls and monkey howls and elephant trumpets masked their own embarrassing noises.

Nina and Karissa had been friends since kindergarten, but, as a result of Nina's family moving to a different district in the middle of her eighth-grade year, they attended different high schools. Their solution to this nonconsensual severing was to get an annual pass to the park. It was about equal distance between their houses and it took the guesswork out of what to do on the weekends.

The boys at the park were different from the boys at their schools. They were mostly from places like Garden Grove or Santa Ana, places nobody ever went on purpose. They wore their pants low and walked with fake limps, had tattoos and stretched earlobes and an air of ambivalence.

Karissa and Nina both knew exactly how long the ride was, anticipated each curve and gentle slope of the track. At about minute one, the car jolted to a stop in front of a cheetah hidden among the foliage—fangs bared, eyes shooting red light, jerking up on enormous hind legs—and then began to pick up speed, past the warning hoot of an owl, two vultures on a wire, wings spread, talons flashing, about to descend. This was where the ride became completely dark. Nothing but jostle of track, cold

breeze, and a growl that struck fear in even the most cou-
rageous child heart.

This was also the point where whatever boy would be-
come the most daring. When a sweaty hand crept up your
skirt. Or you would finally touch it, that first electric jolt
as the boy sucked in breath, so soft and hard at the same
time. About a twenty-second window before the car was
awash in light.

Karissa and Nina smoked the same kind of cigarettes: Parlia-
ment Lights. *P-Funk*, Nina called them. They only smoked
at the park. They only wore big chunky earrings at the park
and dark red lipstick that had to be constantly reapplied
and low-cut shirts they bought together from the Ross
Dress For Less. They'd change in the bathroom in front of
the entrance, doing each other's eye makeup under the flu-
orescent lights and challenging each other to ask a certain
boy, reach a further base. They called it *scamming*. As in,
Are you going to scam him tonight? They only flirted at the
park, only talked trash. Only strutted. Only drank alcohol,
furtively sipped from some boy's flask.

When they got off the ride, there was rumor of a fight, a
girl they'd met at the park, Marina, and another girl who'd
either lit her bangs on fire or made out with her boyfriend.
They all gathered by the Safari Chase.

Nina leaned in to tell Karissa about the coyotes. Her
hair brushed Nina's cheek, smell of cigarette smoke, dusk,
and Pantene. There was something she needed to tell her,
something urgent, but it fluttered up and out like one of
the bats that nested in summer above the gift shop. Instead,
she whispered about Jay's braces. She pulled on her lip to
show the raw part on the inside of her cheek. Karissa was

impressed and a little grossed out. She pretended not to care
that Jarrod was talking to Emily, that Emily was laughing
like he'd just told her a very funny private joke, possibly
raunchy, and was he going ask her to go on the ride with
him because he had already asked Karissa before the whole
drama with Marina and this other girl even happened so
what-the-fuck. Nina said that Emily had bad skin, that
Taylor said her nipples smelled like broccoli, but Karissa
wasn't convinced. She had a tongue ring. Some people said
she'd gone all the way.

Marina and the other girl talked it out with very lit-
tle fanfare, just a barely audible *cunt* and some halfhearted
spitting.

Jarrod was pale and pretty with impeccable fashion sense,
and Karissa had decided to let him put his finger inside her.
This was something other boys had tried, something Nina
had let both Jay and Brian do, but she herself had never
seen the appeal in it. Jarrod was different. Even though she
didn't really know anything about him, he had an ethereal
kind of self-containment, like a seashell's silky spiral.

Nina said it was like putting a tampon in, but Karissa
hadn't done that either. Then she said it was like that feel-
ing when you're running and you think you have to stop
but you push past the burning and then you feel high, and
Karissa knew exactly what she was talking about though
had her doubts about the comparison.

Nina's first kiss was on the ride, a boy with a mustache
named Steve. Rumor was he'd already graduated high
school. His mouth tasted like onions and there had been
altogether too much saliva, but he had soft lips and he
touched the back of her head gently with his fingertips

like he was touching something unbelievably precious and fragile.

She and Karissa saved up details and shared them at the end of the night. Too much tongue, too little tongue, tongue thick and sweet like taffy, hesitant tips of tongue, tongue inscribing careful circles, tongue like a snake reaching for the back of the throat.

At home, Karissa's mother had begun to sulk around the house. She came home from dates slightly drunk telling Karissa the details before carrying her own body up the stairs like a woman twice her age. This one was fifty pounds heavier than his picture; this one talked about himself all night; this one propositioned her with money; this one used to be in jail; this one never finished college; this one talked about his cat all night; this one didn't try to kiss her; this one left early; this one shaved his entire body; this one yelled at the waiter. She had very little time left, her mother said. She was almost at the end of her window. She, Karissa, didn't know how lucky she was, to be at the beginning. But she gave Karissa a look that didn't make her feel lucky at all. What did he say about the cat? Karissa wanted to know. Why would he shave his entire body? But her mother was already kicking off her shoes, already groping the banister.

Nina liked to remember the first time she went on this ride. The thrilling dark. Those animal eyes blinking their hunger, the chirps and howls of a wild world. And instead of some groaning groping boy it was her father, his strong arm against hers. They made up stories. The monkeys were planning a surprise party. The cheetah searched for his long-lost love. How he lightly teased her when she jumped as the cat reared. Now her father worked late hours and had a suspicious glow. Now he looked at her sometimes across the breakfast table like she was a stray that had wandered in. The other night, one of the rare ones when he was home before she left the house, he asked her what they did at the amusement park. "We go on the rides," she'd answered him. "Aren't you tired of those rides?" he asked. But she took that as a rhetorical question and decided to wait for Karissa's sister outside.

Nina and Karissa had become more and more daring on the ride. Pushing against the boundaries of the dark, of the fake animals in their biologically questionable habitats, the watchful gazes that, emptied of life, were like an inducement to live, to indulge the body with its beating heart and intricate branching of nerve endings, its skin and eyes and hunger. Nina and Karissa would push and push until something pushed back. Neither wanted to be the one to hesitate. Both were afraid of what they were building to, whatever that was—oblivion.

At school, if he went to her school, Jarrod wouldn't talk to Karissa, she knows this, knows he wouldn't waste his time with the quiet track girl, would concentrate his efforts on one of the prettier edgier girls who hung out behind the gym building up a repertoire of cool. So as the car coasted into the meadow, her heart sank. This was the first time they'd been on the ride together, not long enough for him to know what a good kisser she was. And he hadn't even tried to unbutton her pants yet. What if he never asked her again? Out of the corner of her eye, she thought she saw a furry thing dart. But when she looked, there was just the lone wolf (wasn't that his usual place along the banister?)

and as they came to a stop the bar raised, the bored teenager manning the ride staring at his phone, not paying attention to them. Jarrod leaned in, hot-breathed and husky-voiced, and asked her to go again.

Nina reached out to touch it as the ride came to an abrupt stop. This happened. Sometimes it was a mechanical failure they had to check or fix or get the okay to ignore; sometimes who knew? Nina suspected the creeps running the ride just liked to watch them, to see what they did in the dark when it stopped. There were cameras everywhere, if you knew where to look, camouflaged in the foliage and behind the quiet anemic stars.

The wolf's fur was soft. She stood up and leaned over the banister, feeling the fine hairs of its ears. Its nose, warm and wet. She wondered how they got it to stay like that. Beside her, Tadd looked uncomfortable. Like he wanted to tell her not to do what she was doing but also wanted to put his hand up her shirt.

She slid her finger inside the wolf's mouth. Slick knobby grooves along the gum line, incisors smoothed to sharp points. She saw dark wet forests, felt her heart thud with the chase. A growl oozed like honey up her throat.

The ride jolted to a start again, and Nina almost lost her balance. And then she did lose her balance. She went over the bar into coarse desert sand. It was a soft fall, but she'd gone over her wrist. Pain shot up her arm. She watched as Tadd stood inside the car, looking like he really wanted to do something, then sat again as the ride jerked around the corner. Two owls with eyes like glowing coal accused her from a rock, something slithered through the sand. The wolf, she could have sworn, crouched.

A different kind of howl interrupted Karissa's make-out session with Jarrod. Reluctantly she pulled away and looked behind them to where the sound had come from, though now all she could hear was the screeching of monkeys. When the car turned the corner she was provided a glimpse of Nina two dioramas back, crumpled among alien desert flowers.

Karissa called to her, but she didn't respond. Tadd, still in the car behind them, looked embarrassed.

"What happened?" she yelled at him, and he shrugged helplessly.

She looked at Jarrod but he, too, seemed to want nothing to do with this. He wiped his mouth with the back of his hand and looked to where the cheetah's eyes were already burning through the darkness.

At school, Karissa walked with her head down. She never spoke in class. She wore her hair long over one side of her face. Her primary goal to take up as little space as possible. Everyone else moved so easily, knew what to do, when she was always too aware of her own body, the parts of it like a board game someone has taken out and forgotten how to play. As she walked down the halls she would sometimes think *elbow elbow elbow* and everything would fuzz over, become strange and threatening. The only time she felt okay at school was on the track. Then her body became machine and a delicious burn began in her legs and swirled upward, turning her into pure movement.

Karissa ran beside the tracks, climbed over the bars. She ran across Styrofoam snow, past the polar bear's heroic bulk, hopped the flickering foil river. Two tusked pigs came dashing from the brush, but Karissa kicked them out of the way and swung into the desert on a hanging wire.

Nina was still lying in the sand. The wolf was less than a foot away from her though still inanimate, thank god. Nina raised herself on one elbow and Karissa crouched beside her. It struck her then: Nina was the most beautiful girl she'd ever known. Sand in her hair, lipstick on her teeth. Karissa reached out and pulled Nina to her feet.

The wolf moved. They both saw it at the same time. One paw, one step forward. A slight crouch. Lip snarled up over its teeth. They could see the furrows in the fur above his nose, the freckle root of his whiskers, the steam from his mouth.

Karissa knelt down and told Nina to get on her back, and then she ran as fast as she could to the exit, through desert and icescape and forest and jungle, screeches and howls at their backs. Karissa's legs burned. Talons scraped Nina's scalp.

Right before the last turn, the elephant stomped into their path, kicking up whorls of polymer snow, unfurling its trunk with a grand trumpeting. Karissa stopped. There was no way around the enormous animal. The elephant lifted a foot, then put it back down. The girls looked into its grandmotherly eyes. Nina slowly put out a hand and touched its dusty trunk, gently rubbed its dusty gray skin, and it blinked its wrinkled lids and stepped aside.

The newspapers called it a malfunction. A faulty gear, freak electrical blitz. They said a car went off the tracks, a couple teenagers fooling around. Nobody ever confronted Nina or Karissa about what happened, though they must have caught it all on tape. The park closed down the ride after that night for several months, and when it finally reopened, it was a completely different ride, one with spinning cups.

The two girls never told anyone, never talked about it again. That night, as they huddled together in the cold and waited for Karissa's sister to pick them up, as Nina drank an entire half flask of whiskey Jay gave her for the pain, the most they could do was exchange looks of disbelief and gratitude.

They were both forbidden to return to the park. Nina's father maintained an attitude that suggested he thought her wrist injury, what turned out to be a minor sprain, was somehow self-inflicted. The two girls tried to still hang out on the weekends, the movies, the mall. But it wasn't the same. Like being in black and white after knowing color. And then Karissa's mother met and married a handsome unshaven architect from Washington, and they moved at the end of the year. The two girls wrote to each other, though life got complicated, and the letters became less and less frequent. As they got older, the memory of that strange encounter faded, a watercolor folded into a drawer.

Funnel cake and cigarette smoke. Strobing lights from the Whirlibird. The feeling of eyes, zigzag of roped-off lanes. Hard benches. The zebra sharing a shady spot underneath a tree with the white tiger. The eagle riding on the back of the rhino. Cherry lip gloss. That total blackness before the meadow. A boy's cool hand on the back of your neck, the whir and click of electronic cicadas. Tin sinks and powder soap. Stuffing our bras with toilet paper. What we wrote in endless loops over the stall doors. *Nina + Karissa forever.*

Fall from Grace

The first one, a visitor from out of town, slipped on a mossy rock and fell one thousand feet into the gorge's open mouth. Then Marcy Eldritch, a week from her thirteenth birthday, leaned too far out a third-floor window. The neighbor broke his neck, lost his balance cleaning his gutters. Ten people dropped twenty floors when an elevator cable broke in the bank building downtown.

They keep falling. One after another. City officials are hesitant to call it an epidemic, but the media has no such qualms. Details are sensationalized, distance hyperbolized. It seems all anyone talks about these days. At the grocery store, in line at the post office. *Did you hear about the dentist, the window cleaner, the taxidermist, the baker who slipped on the ice, stepped over the precipice, the scaffolding, lip of the well?*

Not all falls are fatal. Most are doing it more often: tripping on shoelaces, cracks in the sidewalk, showing up for work with scabs, bruises, Band-Aids across chins and noses and knees, wincing.

My wife says it's a hex. She believes in witches, my wife. Baba Yaga in her little hut on chicken feet. Someone in this town, my wife won't point fingers, *did something*.

All this seems like a steep price to pay for one person's mistake. But I guess who knows, all you can do is be extra careful. Keep antibiotic ointment on hand. Avoid high places.

Three teachers from the elementary school fall off their Vespas. A three-year-old falls into the lion exhibit at the zoo. Dr. Wheeler, who is not a real doctor but is very good at fixing bikes, falls from the climbing wall at the gym. My wife keeps falling out of bed. I wake to the familiar *kathump* then theatrical groan as she crawls back under the sheets.

I have my own theories. Because people have lost all sense of what's real. What's important. But maybe our souls, or whatever you want to call the part that speaks in dreams, what attaches us to the universe, to the stars and the antelopes, know better. Maybe they throw our bodies down to humble us, to remind us what the ground feels like, to remind us of these bodies.

But some of us already know. Some of us are already so in our bodies these days they throb at the slightest touch.

My confession is that I feel lighter. I haven't fallen once. While everyone around me plummets, while my wife tumbles from stairs and curbs and nothing at all, flat ground, while the bruises drift like shadow continents beneath her skin, I remain intact, upright. Buoyant, even.

I begin to test my luck, just to see what the limits are. I lean over extravagantly high balconies, climb tall trees, take my dinners on the roof. What does it mean to fall from grace, to fall behind, to fall apart? What does it mean to fall in love?

Lean back, my wife says, holding out her arms behind me, *I'll catch you.*

All Men

1.

You live in a certain kingdom in a certain land with your mother and sister. Your sister is tall and beautiful with the voice of a songbird. Though not as beautiful, you are fierce with exceptional hand-eye coordination. You can throw your dagger and pierce an enemy's heart from a hundred feet away. Or at least you could, if given the opportunity.

Before he died, your father made some people angry, and these people (men, let's be honest, of course they were all men), often blinded by gold—literally, as a result of your father's alchemical ineptitude—promised your father and his family vengeance. Though these threats have proved mostly empty, you remain vigilant. You practice with your dagger on tree trunks and apples and socks stuffed with straw.

The slice of arrow through air, plunge of your dagger into soft belly, surprise in the enemy's eyes that your face is the last he sees (or, if he's blind, the faltering recognition of your scent, a combination, your sister says, of mushrooms, cedar chips, and moonlight)—while your sister talks of love and roses, of dashing knights and romantic trysts, ideas she gets from novels the covers of which are frayed and curled from a long history of matrilineal readings, you fantasize about this.

One day, your mother becomes ill. It happens fast. She's pale and coughs blood. The doctor comes, but it's too late. Before she dies, your mother tells you and your sister that two suitors will arrive, that she has read it in her tea leaves, that you must marry them: They are your destiny and will keep you safe.

But I can keep us safe, you say.

Of course you can, my dear, she says. But love is a special kind of safe. It protects more than your body. It protects your soul.

Protects it from what?

From—influences.

You don't ask her what influences. You know them. They are woven into the stories she has told you and your sister since you could remember. Stories, mostly, of Baba Yaga, the witch of the woods. Both warning and thrill. A warning of what happens to a woman alone, the ugliness and corruption. The thrill of a dangerous story (is there any other kind?). Sometimes Baba Yaga has a long bony nose and wears a housedress dyed with the bark of cypress trees. Sometimes she lives in a hut that stands on chicken feet in the middle of the forest, its walls barely able to contain her long dangly body. Sometimes she flies around in a mortar, holding a broom and pestle, sweeping her way up, erasing her traces. Sometimes she has helpers—bodiless hands, the three horsemen, a magic firebird. But always she tricks. Impels young girls into the deep part of the woods. Gives them impossible tasks. Sets ungenerous terms.

I'm not afraid of Baba Yaga, you say.

Have I taught you nothing? your mother says.

Though most of your mother's tea-leaf predictions never materialize, shortly after her funeral suitors do, in fact, arrive, as raven and eagle, great powerful birds that swoop and soar and then reassemble as a handsome prince and dashing knight.

If you decide to marry the eagle prince, go to 2. If you decide to go find the man you suspect of poisoning your mother, go to 3.

2.

You and the eagle prince are happy. His palace is full of beautiful things, woodwork the prince has done himself, chairs and tables and cabinets carved with elaborate scenes, his-eye views of forests and mountains and men, velvet draped over every surface, prisms in the windows that shift rainbows over the floor. The prince himself is gentle and charming. He keeps you entertained with stories of the people of the kingdom with equal parts compassion and gossip; he draws you long hot baths; and, though he only shows them to you at the peak of passion, his wings are soil-dark, alive with oily feathers, and he arcs them over you, a hole with no center.

But still, after some time, a short time or a long time, you become restless. You miss practicing with your dagger. You miss your sister. If you decide to go try to find one of your father's enemies, go to 3. If you decide to go visit your sister, go to 4.

3.

You'd heard that Koschei the Deathless—before your father died, his primary enemy—is vacationing on the coast. Your plan is to take him by surprise, before he has the chance to go after you or your sister. Your plan doesn't extend too much beyond this, but you trust your instincts; you think well on your feet. Besides, if you're honest with yourself, the challenge is your primary motivation, the thrill of trying to kill someone who doesn't die, and being without a plan only increases this thrill.

At the coast you ask around about Koschei the Death-less's whereabouts. The townspeople are strangely evasive. When they respond—*Koschei the what?*—they look over their shoulder, spit surreptitiously into their hand. But you are not deterred. You go to the local watering hole and wait. Koschei the Deathless, like many immortal villains, enjoys a good bourbon, neat, in the company of faceless strangers (the faceless, like the deathless, tend to congregate near the sea). So you take a seat at the bar, order a beer. You don't have to wait very long. Koschei the Deathless walks in just as you've taken the first sip, tall and skinny in his black trench coat and greasy hair, his pockmarked face, AC/DC T-shirt. He sits on the other side of the bar, orders his bour-bon with his eyes, and wearily takes a drink.

Koschei the Deathless meets your gaze. He smiles. He clearly does not recognize you.

Nice to see a face around here, he says. And a pretty one at that.

You thank him and flex your calf, feeling the reassur-ing sheath of your dagger beneath your boot. You begin to doubt yourself, begin to doubt your motivations. You re-member the story your father told you. Deathless had hired your father to turn his heart to gold, the only way Koschei the Deathless could cheat his fate, the only way Death could finally find him. Koschei the Deathless had enjoyed hundreds of deathless years so far, and he'd grown tired, tired of the pettiness of people, the same small-heartedness again and again, generation after generation. He'd never found love after all that time, the same woman, vapid and self-involved and not able to see beyond her small life—it was time, he was ready to finally leave this world. But your father, after making him stand to his shoulders in cow dung for two hours, proved unable to accomplish this feat. So

Deathless had doubled down, dedicated his life to immortal debauchery and vowed to exact revenge on your family.

You don't know how he did it, and maybe he didn't. All you know is that the day before your mother became sick, your sister swore she saw him, a flash of greasy hair in the apple orchard.

Deathless offers to buy you a drink.

If you accept the drink, go to 5. If you decide to ask Deathless to step outside, go to 6.

4.

Your sister and the raven knight live in Colorado at the top of a mountain where it is perpetually snowing. Their house is made entirely of glass, and your sister has upholstered all the furniture in white linen, which sits on a carpet of stitched-together polar bear coats (procured, she assures you, through sustainable means). Your sister looks happy. She has always been quiet and somewhat withdrawn, and this new life seems to suit her, beautiful and sharp and glittering.

The raven knight cracks nuts for her and brings her shiny things, ricochets kindness in the manner of a deep and uncomplicated canyon. But still, there's something not quite right, you think. Like, maybe he's *too nice*.

Just because you like that rough, top-predator kind of love, doesn't mean I have to, she says.

I just want you to be happy.

I am happy.

Maybe *happy* should not be the goal.

You said you want me to be happy.

That's just something people say when they love you. What I meant was, I want you to be fully alive, to feel the moon pull the tides of your blood. I want you to have orgasms and sing and throw plates.

I have orgasms.

You look at her.

What? I do. At least I think I do.

Come on, you say, throwing your sister her coat. We're going to have an adventure.

Where are we going?

It's a surprise, you say.

If you take your sister to the coast, go to 8. If you take her to the forest, go to 7.

5.

Why don't you take your boots off? Koschei the Death-less asks.

After a couple drinks, you'd followed him back to his place, a dingy beach house that smells like wet dog. You've already let him put his cold sharp-nailed finger inside you while inexpertly licking your nipples. You've had enough. You lift your leg, offering up your boot. As he unlaces it, your dagger loosens from where it had sat snug against your calf, and you reach out and grab hold, watching his face as your fingers close around the handle, the recognition as you plunge the blade deep into his belly.

This is just my body, he says, looking in astonishment at the blood leaking from his abdomen. You have to find my soul.

If you step outside to try to clear your head, go to 6. If you say fuck this noise and decide to take a trip with your sister instead, go to 7.

6.

The air is cool and smells of the sea. The sun has disappeared but it is not yet dark. You hear your mother's voice telling you the story of Koschei the Deathless. *He cannot be killed*

by traditional methods, you hear her say. His soul is not in-
side his body. It is inside a needle, which is inside an egg,
which is inside a duck, which is inside a hare, which is in-
side an iron chest buried under an oak tree on the island of
Buyan. If you find and open this chest, the hare will run.
If killed, the duck will be freed and try to fly off. If cap-
tured, the duck will eventually lay its egg. If you break the
needle, Koschei will die.

That is way too complicated, you tell your mother's voice
inside your head. I think I'm over it. I have to get back to the
eagle prince. I gave up top-predator sex for what, for this?

You feel Deathless behind you, but when you turn
around, there is no one. The only sign of life an old lady
across the street walking a dog.

The old woman crosses the street, and as she gets
nearer, you see that she is not walking a dog, that it is in
fact a chicken. You recognize her. She recognizes you. The
chicken squawks.

Suddenly Koschei the Deathless is behind you; he sweeps
you up in his cold thin arms and forces you back into his
place. He takes you down into his basement. Though he's
removed your dagger from his abdomen, blood continues
to leak from him, turning the paler parts of the image on
his shirt, AC/DC's Malcolm Young ripping on his guitar,
a wet, almost pretty pink.

You can't get away from me, baby, Deathless says, a lit-
tle out of breath. We're fate.

If dying is what you want, why are you trying so hard
to escape it? you ask.

Koschei the Deathless shrugs. I guess we don't always
know what we want.

You hear something familiar, a keening kind of screech.
The eagle prince flies through the high basement window.

He's never looked so regal or so dashing, your eagle prince, as he unfolds his soil-dark wings and bends to you. Deathless watches, speechless, as he takes you on his back and flies off.

However, Deathless has a horse with wings that outpaces him, and he recaptures you. This happens another time. The eagle prince saves you, Koschei the Deathless recaptures you. And again. Finally, sick of being captured and saved and captured and saved, you tell the eagle prince to go get a faster horse from Baba Yaga.

7.

You lead your sister down the mountain, into the forest. It's quiet and dark and smells like electricity. You follow a path that appears well-trod.

As soon as you are about to turn back—your sister has become apprehensive, she's cold and hungry and it's getting dark, darker—you come upon it: Baba Yaga's hut. Rather unassuming from the outside, your basic wood-and-moss affair.

Are you crazy? your sister asks.

I don't think Mother told us everything, you say. I want to see Baba Yaga for myself. Her hut looks nothing like the stories. No glowing skulls on spikes, no human teeth in the door lock. No chicken feet.

I'm not going in there, your sister says.

Fine, you say. Then I'll go by myself.

But your sister follows you up the steps, as you knew she would. Because she doesn't like to be alone, and because she loves you.

As you walk in, Baba Yaga is backlit, bent over her sewing, a mass of black wool. She is not ten feet tall folded into her hut like a jack-in-the-box. But she is not little by any means. The size of a woman who is tired of not taking up space.

Did you come of your own free will, or did someone send you? She asks while keeping her eyes on her handiwork. None of the screech-and-wail of the stories.

We come of our own free will, Mother.

Then come in. Come closer. Let me take a look at you.

You and your sister come in and stand before Baba Yaga. The door closes behind you. The effect of her is a gathering of the elements. Hair long and silver and full of electricity. Her eyes are the gray of storm clouds. Her skin is bark, weathered and wrinkled and alive.

You can hear the voice of your mother, whipping the strands of the fairy tales into a larger whole, a fluffy meringue of story. The one where Baba Yaga tried to trick Vasilisa the Beautiful by giving her impossible tasks to complete, sorting grains of rice, washing poppy seeds, threatening to eat her if she did not complete them.

The Maiden Tsar's love inside the egg inside the duck inside the hare, how Baba Yaga gave Ivan the firebird. The merchant's daughter, who tricks Baba Yaga and her daughters by pretending not to know how to lie on the roasting pan to fit in the oven. Show me how, she says. And they do.

Stories with haphazard logic. All going deep into the woods. All talking birds and counting spoons, death and love hiding in eggs in ducks in hares. Where integrity, bravery, and cleverness are rewarded. But always the terms are uncertain. The rules change based on the whims of Baba Yaga.

After some time, a short time, or a long time.

What do you want? Baba Yaga asks you now.

Your sister looks at you. You look at her. You both look at Baba Yaga. Was there something you wanted?

Baba Yaga sighs. If you want to find Koschei the Deathless, she says, go to 3. If you want to follow me deeper into the woods, go to 9.

8.

At the coast, you try to avoid the bar on the main drag, the one with the faceless woman outlined in neon above the door. Your sister was never much of a drinker anyway. Instead, the two of you take ice cream cones—your sister's bubble gum, yours chocolate-chocolate chip—down to the water.

Koschei the Deathless is likely in The Silent Lady at that very moment, notorious for his bourbon habit and seducing the promiscuous faceless for which that particular hole-in-the-wall is known.

As you walk along the shoreline, the ice cream sweet and cold with a promise of diminishing returns, as it grows sticky at your wrist and the water foams at your toes and your sister chatters on about the addition she and the raven knight are building off the back deck, it's difficult to remain one hundred percent in the moment. Part of you is thinking about the dagger you have hidden in your boot. It presses in its sheath against the outside of your shin, a pressure that rides up your calf and upper thigh, settles somewhere in the deep end of your spine.

This is so good, your sister says, her tongue and lips blue.

You look like a true ice princess, you say.

Your sister blows a big bubble and you put your finger through it.

Is this our adventure? she asks.

You look out at the endless water. The blank sand. The sky without a cloud. A faceless woman is playing with a little boy with too much face, cheeks obscenely chubby, lips fat as slugs. The two of them move piles of dry sand around.

Yeah, this is pretty lame, you say.

No it's nice, your sister says. She laces her sticky fingers through yours. I'm glad we did this. I miss you.

Do you ever feel like you're meant for something more?

More than what?

You look into her clear uncomplicated blue eyes. The little boy with a surplus of face runs into the ocean squealing and his mother reaches out her hands as if to catch him but doesn't get up.

If you go back to the hotel, wait for your sister to go to sleep, and then try to find Koschei the Deathless at the bar, go to 3. If you take your sister to the forest to continue your adventure, go to 7.

9.

Your sister decided to go back to the hotel, and so you follow Baba Yaga through the woods by yourself, farther and farther, until the trees grow so tall they block out the sun and the ground becomes soft at your feet. Eventually you reach Baba Yaga's hut, the real one, made of wood and moss standing on chicken legs twenty feet tall, thick around as tree trunks and covered in yellow scaly skin. Teeth, what look to be human teeth, in the lock on the door. Around the hut is a white picket fence that, when you get closer, you realize is topped with human skulls, bleached white by the sun. You attempt to remain calm and not think about who the skulls belonged to before they were shorn of skin and life and how they ended up here. Baba Yaga has not spoken to you the entire journey. You are still not sure whether she intends to kill you or help you. From the stories, you know that Baba Yaga is quick to anger but also respects moxie and the pure of heart.

The chicken feet bend, the hut's door opens, and still Baba Yaga doesn't so much as turn around. As you step up into the hut, you begin to think this was a very bad idea. You can't remember what possessed you to leave your handsome eagle prince, your hand-carved furnishings. You hear your mother's words. *Be happy with what you have, dear child. Don't go looking for trouble.*

Please take a seat, Baba Yaga says. Now I must ask you. Did you come here of your own free will, or did someone send you?

You told me to follow you.

Do you always do what people tell you to do?

Your fingers itch for the dagger in your boot but you know she would kill you with a look before you even had a chance to remove it. Are you going to kill me? you ask.

I am going to give you a test. If you pass, I will give you your freedom along with a gift to take back to your eagle prince. If you fail, you will remain here with me. Forever.

What if I don't agree to these terms?

We always have a choice. Though the consequences of that choice are often out of our control.

Fine. What is the test?

Baba Yaga reaches under the table and pulls out a piece of paper along with a number two pencil. She passes the paper and the pencil to you. It is a multiple choice test made up of ten questions.

The first one is: Chickens can live for how long with their heads cut off?

If you answer **A**, Eighteen months, go to 10. If you answer **D**, A few minutes, go to 1.

10.

I'm sorry, Baba Yaga says, but you've gotten one of these wrong.

That's impossible, you say. Which one?

I can't tell you that.

Was it the one about the chicken? Because I just read a story about a chicken in Colorado that survived for eighteen months after his head was cut off. I swear. His name was Mike. Mike the headless chicken.

You shouldn't believe everything you read, Baba Yaga says. She takes down the silver dreadlocks piled on top of her head and they coil around her bony shoulders like snakes.

You feel the room shift, the uneasy tilt of chicken feet scratching in the dirt.

Baba Yaga puts her feet up on the table, her legs and arms seeming so much longer now, growing, reaching almost to the walls.

But wait, you say. You're a woman. I'm a woman. Women should stick together. It's tough enough out there.

But we are sticking together, Baba Yaga says. Trust me, this is the happiest ending you're gonna get. You better sharpen that dagger, child. I got a long list of people who've pissed me off over the years. Men. Let's be honest, they're all men. Inept, weak, lazy. Cryin' for their mommas. And don't worry, Koschei the Deathless is at the very top of it.

As you feel the chicken feet pick up speed, you glance out the window to see the eagle prince. He glides along the tops of the trees, calling you with his top-predator screech. He looks so regal, so dashing. All you would have to do is run to the window.

You lock eyes with Baba Yaga. Her hair begins to spark. She grins, dark gaping holes where most of her teeth should be, big crooked nose, breasts loose and swinging.

Hold on, she says. She runs better than she flies, but it's gonna be a bumpy ride.

The Rapture Index

"Do you think we should be more worried?" I ask. "Should we take him to someone?" I nod to where Jeremy sits in the sand.

Henry shoves in the last of his hot dog and grunts, shakes his head no. Ketchup squeezes out the side of his mouth.

"When I went over, he was drawing those crosses again. When I asked him to join us, he put up his finger, like he was deep in the middle of something and couldn't be bothered." I think about looking through the basket for napkins but decide the basket is too far away.

Henry was the one to organize this picnic at the beach, saying we needed to *spend some QT as a family.* He insists on these outings every few months—so we can check in with each other, inspect for damage, melancholy, make sure everything's intact.

Henry wipes his mouth with the back of his hand, smearing a ketchup shadow up the side of his cheek. "He's a kid. Kids get caught up in stuff. He's just trying to figure out who he is, become an individual."

I hate when he says things like that, like he knows everything about raising a child, surprised I haven't read the manual. "But why religion? He certainly didn't get that from us. Where did he even have access to it? It scares me, to think he won't think. He needs to be able to think. What about college?"

Henry looks at me like I'm being silly. I haven't told him about the cat paw. A week ago Jeremy ran in from the yard holding the severed paw of Mrs. Greenwood's tabby. Coyotes had been coming down from the hills into the canyon's surrounding neighborhoods, getting into trash and taking pets. The Flahertys down the street had lost their Shih Tzu the week before.

Jeremy held out the paw like a find, a cool leaf or rock. Without thinking, I grabbed it from him. It was still soft, the tabby's unmistakable brown and black striped fur, her white paw. Where it had been separated from the cat, blood had dried a crusty rust, knob of bone jutting from the dirty fur. I wrapped it in a garbage bag and shoved it in the trash bin behind the house. I didn't tell Mrs. Greenwood, whose cat had been missing for weeks. I didn't tell Henry. When I asked Jeremy where he'd found the paw, he shrugged.

"In the backyard."

"Why did you pick it up?" I asked him.

"God told me to."

Oh no, I thought. *Here we go.* At some level I'd been dreading a moment like this ever since Jeremy was born. A good boy, sweet and considerate and smart. His teachers love him, friends are always amazed how well-behaved he is, *just like a little adult*. Picked out his own clothes since he was four: brown or gray slacks (at five he learned to iron them so the crease shows), button-down shirt, always tucked in—the same outfit he still wears, at eleven. Always in the accelerated reading group in school, he has taken from our shelves and read *Moby Dick*, *The Sun Also Rises*, even some of Henry's thick medical texts.

"What do you mean God told you to?" I asked. "Are you hearing voices?"

Jeremy shook his head. "Just God's."

"It's going to rain," Henry says. I look up and, as if on cue, it starts to come down, cold fat drops. We're both in sleeveless shirts and shorts. Thunder cracks directly overhead.

"Come on Jeremy, let's go," I call, and when he doesn't respond I run over, grab his hand, pull him to his feet. He giggles. For some reason he loves being pulled at, tugged. The crosses are still there, oversized dollar store crucifixes carved in the sand, but he's also drawn some kind of animal, lines curving in elegant arcs toward the water. Maybe it'll be art he'll get into next, I think, something I could understand, something we could share.

"Could be the end," Jeremy says on our way to the car.

"It's not the end of the world, Jeremy, it's a thunder shower." I try not to sound annoyed.

"I know." He grabs my hand. "I know the difference."

"I'm sorry." I hold his hand up to my nose and sniff. He smells different today, pungent. "Your dad been giving you beef jerky again?"

He shakes his head and climbs into the backseat of the car while I put the picnic basket in the trunk. Henry's picking up the last of our stuff, throwing away paper plates and soda cans, when there's a heavy metallic thud, and I look up in time to see him crumple to the ground. I fight the urge to laugh: the awkward twist of Henry's body, his shrill yelp. Because he slips often, sometimes on dry carpet—as steady as his hands might be with other's bones, at home his body goes loose and clumsy—I've learned not to make a big deal out of his falls. But when he doesn't get up, I run back to the picnic table.

There's blood on his forehead and his eyes are closed, I can't tell if he's breathing. I panic, put my mouth on his and try to force breath into him. I begin pumping his chest, trying to remember from a CPR class I'd taken in college, was it four beats, breathe, repeat? But if Henry lost consciousness it was just for a moment; he pushes against my shoulders and moans, opening his eyes. When I ask if I should call an ambulance, he shakes his head.

"I hate those assholes," he says, squinting up at me. His smile is a grimace, but his eyes look clear.

At the hospital they run MRI and CT scans, but they don't find anything permanent, just a surface wound that requires a couple stitches. Roy Mannette, a neurologist Henry had gone to school with, says Henry is fine.

"Well, you just missed the middle meningeal artery, no temporal bone fracturing," he says, tapping his pencil's chewed eraser on the scan of Henry's brain: a flat etched shadow, weathered sand dollar. "Honestly Henry, you should thank your lucky stars. If you had hit your head that hard a little to the right, you'd probably be dead." He winks at me. I've never liked Roy very much. All the times I've had to suffer through a boring dinner party trying to follow all the ways he's saved someone's life—he's stolen whole hours of *my* life.

I reach out and put a hand on Henry's knee. "Well that's good news, right?"

He chuckles like I've told a clever joke, and then kisses me on the cheek.

"You should come over," he says to Roy. "It's been a while. Bring Penny, we'll eat and drink—defy death."

In the car on the way home, I ask Henry if he's feeling OK. He stares out at the other cars we're stopped beside in traffic. In the backseat Jeremy holds the image of Henry's perfectly intact brain up to the window. The rain has stopped and the streets are already dry. On the radio a woman talks about the still-arid conditions around the Santa Monica hills.

"Yeah." He rolls up the window and turns off the radio. "Do you hear that?"

"Hear what?" I try to listen but there isn't anything, the engine perfectly silent.

"That music."

"I don't hear anything, Henry. Maybe it's another car, bass."

"No, it's still there, like hmm, hm, hmmm, hm hm hm."

I shake my head. "Something's probably just loose in there, you knocked your head pretty good."

Henry stares out the window. "It's beautiful," he whispers.

A week after the accident, I'm in the back room framing a piece that just arrived. It's a large oil painting of an industrial plant. Bold phallic shapes and an absence of color, desolate and arrogant. I think of Henry, the humming that kept me awake last night—he's been doing it in his sleep; every time I roll him over he stops, but only for a few minutes. There's something different about him, an energy, his body less disastrous, graceful even.

Our marriage has never been perfect. But in its imperfection, its quiet stasis, I've enjoyed a certain peace. Space. I'd already had my share of wild sex, the body's quick swing from bliss to hatred. That kind of passion only got in the way of the self, left me with less time for me, my work. The gallery was my love affair. And there were a couple artists along the way. A physical, animal exchange. I separated the two, my home and my career.

But lately I can't stop staring at Henry, wanting him. I do stupid, teenage things, tell him about some dumb compliment a buyer gave me, *eyes like sunlight through sea glass,* wear my expensive lacy bras and leave my blouse unbuttoned. I bend down directly in front of him in my tight jeans, fabricating a stubborn sticky spot on the floor.

Henry claims to hear music in his head now, convinced it suddenly means he's a musician. He's bought a six-string guitar and a banjo and spends all his free time practicing. He's awful but I still sit and listen, entranced with his fingers, unable to look away as they carefully press down on the strings, the tips blushing pink.

The phone rings and I look at the painting half-framed and chipped at the corner where I hadn't even noticed I dropped it. I sigh and gently set the painting on the floor, covering the chipped end with some newspaper.

The caller is probably a buyer, but it might be Henry. He might need me. Hurrying to the phone, I trip over one of the cast-iron giraffes we're getting ready to exhibit. The phone stops ringing and the automated message system begins its recitation. I take off my shoe and rub my ankle while my own voice greets someone with a breezy cheer I barely recognize.

It's Jeremy's teacher, Mrs. Sams. She'd like to set up an appointment with Henry and me. There is some concern regarding Jeremy's recent behavior in class.

"Shit, shit, shit," I say out loud. Mrs. Sams wishes me a good afternoon and I press my forehead to one of the giraffe's long cool legs.

I take a deep breath and visualize the industrial plant hanging in the north corner of the gallery, granite frame anchoring it to the immaculate wall, the smell of sulfur and smoke.

"Will you stop messing around on that thing for one minute and help me?" I yell from the living room.

The playing stops. "Be there in a second," Henry calls, continuing to strum off-key. He's been in his study all day practicing his new ukulele.

"Do you want me to break my back? Please." I stand in the bedroom doorway holding one of the living room lamps I'd been trying to place.

"It feels like a triquetral," Henry says, turning the instrument over in his hands. "Delicate, prone to fracture. You have to spend time, figure out its secrets, where it's strong."

"That's interesting, but I need help moving the couch right now."

Henry looks up and plucks at the strings. "You've asked me to help you move the couch five times this week. What's wrong with where it is this time?"

"I don't know, there's still something off. It's making the room feel small and dark. Taking all the oxygen out."

"The couch is taking out oxygen?"

"I don't expect you to understand. Angle and color, placement. They affect us along very crucial pathways."

Jeremy walks into Henry's study and sits next to him on the folded-up futon. I'd almost forgotten he was home. He looks up at Henry, forehead wrinkled, lips set in a hard, worried line.

"Hey there, Jerm," Henry says, "I thought you were outside playing with the kids next door? I thought you were showing them your new football?"

After the phone call from Jeremy's teacher, Henry bought Jeremy a football, even though he'd never expressed any interest. "He just needs to get outside more," Henry said, "run around. This'll pass, he just needs to make a pass," and then he'd laughed, as if hitting his head had made him funny.

Lately Jeremy spends all his time in his room on the computer. He combs the Internet tracking current events for signs of the second coming. I walk into his room at all times of the evening and there he is at his computer, little sweet face intent, aglow. He contributes to a site called The Rapture Index, which apparently computes the end times using a precise mathematical equation. He searches all the major news sources for hurricanes, volcanoes, powerful political leaders, abortion statistics. He brings these things up at the dinner table, or at breakfast, as if it all points clearly to one thing, the end of the world. We've tried to dissuade him from this conclusion, engage him in a Socratic method of inquiry, but his belief is unshakable.

Jeremy reaches up and touches Henry's forehead, where the still-raw divot in his skin is slowly turning into a scar. "The mark of the beast," Jeremy says sadly.

"Jeremy," I say. It feels like I'm always saying his name in this way, the kind of scolding lilt I swore I'd never use with my kids. And there's that familiar odor again, I can't place it, maybe not like beef jerky at all. "Jeremy, when's the last time you took a bath? You don't smell very good."

"Six six six adds up to eighteen. It's what's on your forehead," Jeremy says, tracing the mark with his finger.

"No son, that's where I hit my head. It's just healing."

"Jeremy, not everything is a sign," I say.

Jeremy looks at me with a patient, weary smile—the kind of smile a parent gives a child or a priest gives a sinner. I feel that smile in my gut, this child I'm no longer in control of. Maybe I never had been. He looks back to Henry. "Don't worry, Dad, I'm working on it, I'll fight for you."

"Thanks, buddy," he says. When I look at Henry he's distracted, his concentration back to the ukulele, turning one of the silver knobs at the top of the neck. I get the feeling, not for the first time, that Henry's accident might have done more damage than we realize.

"I'm going outside now," Jeremy says, jumping up and leaving, gone.

"You have to be firmer with him," I say to Henry. "He's getting the message from you this is all alright, that his behavior is acceptable. You're turning me into the strict cold parent."

"Come on. He's not really doing anything, I mean we can't punish him for practicing his religion, it goes against everything this country stands for." He grins and I smile back, though I don't want to. Henry runs his thumb along the strings of the ukulele. "My / dog / has / fleas," he sings. "I think the last string is off."

I take a deep breath and let it out slowly. "Fine. Just don't forget Wednesday night we're meeting with Jeremy's teacher. I really think we should both go."

"Sounds good," Henry says, and there's a long silence, my breath burning in my chest.

I set the lamp down and drop to my knees in front of him. I want him with a fierceness that physically hurts, a violent prickling fever. And I hate feeling it, my self, split open for him to see or take or ignore. I yank at his belt, the leather cutting into my hands, pull it tight against his belly. The ukulele is knocked to the floor.

Henry leans over to pick up the instrument. He turns it in his hands, inspecting for damage. I let go of his belt, sit back on my feet, arms limp, a scolded child. There's a crack in the wood at the base of the neck that he probes with his fingers. "Damn," he mutters.

I stand and pick up the lamp. Once I gain control of my breath and step back into the doorway, I feel almost like myself again. "Be ready to go Wednesday at five, we're meeting her at five thirty." Henry looks at me as if I just hurt a small animal. "What? It's not like you don't have a dozen other instruments. I won't be making dinner tonight."

Henry puts the ukulele aside and stares at me. His gaze lingers on my bare shoulders. I wait, hovering in the doorway, the lamp heavy in my hands.

"I wasn't asking you to stop," he says.

I think about putting the lamp down again, what it would take to cross the couple feet to where he's sitting. But for some reason, I can't imagine it, there are too many small actions that would need to be done simultaneously, facial expressions and movements and steps and gestures. An impossible distance.

"I think the moment's passed."

The Santa Monica Mountains are on fire. The fires had started the previous day, suspected arson, dry conditions and Santa Ana winds preventing any kind of containment. It's being fanned into the surrounding housing developments. *Wind-whipped*, the news keeps saying. *The wind-whipped blaze has already destroyed several homes and hundreds of people are being asked to evacuate.* But the images are hazy—a slow-moving orange blur next to fuzzy colors and shapes supposed to be trees and house. Fires spring up in the area every year, but they never reach our home.

I continue rearranging the living room. There's still something not quite right. The room's objects are fine, I picked out all the furniture myself, but somehow over the last couple weeks the mood has shifted—sometimes all it takes is one misplaced thing. I pull the coffee table farther from the couch. Separate the long skinny candles on top of the mantle, place them at opposite ends.

Jeremy is outside; I asked him to rake the lawn in preparation for company. We're entertaining a small gathering of people tomorrow. Henry organized it: a concert. He certainly isn't ready yet, but I'm not going to say it. Things have been strained the last couple days, both of us very polite and serious, making sure we go to bed at separate times, making excuses about dinner.

I don't really care whether the lawn has leaves or not, I like them, the crunch, a reminder of real falls. My childhood, when all the leaves fell off the trees and flew around like bright wings. But I wanted to get Jeremy away from his computer. It's Saturday and he's eleven years old. Henry was right; he should be throwing a football or burning bugs with a magnifying glass or at the very least riding his bike through the streets. Anything but staring at a computer screen, contemplating fire and brimstone.

As I turn one of the floor lamps to face north, I consider my guilt. I can tell just by looking out the window that the air quality is getting worse. I open the door and call for Jeremy. The lawn is swept clean, though leaves continue to fall, faster than the ash. I call his name again. The air is heavy with smoke. Immediately I start coughing. Ash falls like sleepwalking shadows. The sun burns an angry orange dot through the smoke. The whole dirty apricot sky is too low.

I walk to the end of the street and then back up the other side, calling out for Jeremy. Nobody opens their doors, all curtains and shutters closed. Where is everyone?

When I reach the house, I pick up speed. I imagine dialing 911, what I might say: *I've lost my child. I sent him to do yard work in this smoke and he disappeared.* I cough, try to fan the thickness from my face, but there's nowhere else for it to go.

Almost to the front door, I notice a big pile of leaves off to the side of the house, a flash of blue amid all the reds and yellows: Jeremy's baseball cap. I expect the worst: images of him dead, mutilated, buried in the pile of leaves. But he's alive, content as ever, lying in the middle of the leaves with his hands behind his head, looking up at the sky.

"Jeremy," I say, breathless now, too surprised and relieved to yell, "Didn't you hear me calling you?"

Jeremy turns toward me and his eyes are the gold of found treasure, lashes catching flakes of ash. "The sun became as black as sackcloth, and the moon became as blood."

"Jeremy, come on, come inside, it's not healthy out here." I hold out my hand and he takes it.

"He opened the shaft of the bottomless pit, and from the shaft rose smoke like the smoke of a great furnace, and the sun and the air were darkened with the smoke from the shaft."

I pull him up by the arm, probably harder than is necessary, into the house and close the front door behind us. I kneel down and brush the ash from his hair and face. "What am I going to do with you?" I ask him.

He giggles when I blow on his neck and he's a normal little boy again. "Stop it, that tickles."

I sigh, his face between my hands. "Jeremy, this is not the end of the world."

⁘

Out the car window, the browns and yellows blur past. As Henry drives to the school, humming and tapping the steering wheel, I think about inventive paint names that might be involved in this landscape: Peanut Butter and Honey. Muskrat Tea. Princess Hair.

When I was young, I'd tried a brief stint as a painter. Pale, droopy seascapes covered my dorm room walls. But there's a point when you realize you aren't progressing, you don't have that thing you need to be a great artist, and when that happened I gave into it, decided I was better off nurturing others with talent. Sometimes, though, before work when Henry has gone and Jeremy's off at school, I take out my shoebox of watercolors. I mix them together on the blank pages of an old photo album. The color combinations are what interest me. Without form, the colors are simple and uncomplicated, a kind of limitless magma into which I can imagine anything.

"A patient came in yesterday for a distal clavicle excision," Henry says. "I had been the one, months ago, to diagnose the patient, to recommend the procedure. But right before the surgery, I kept rolling those words around in my head, and they didn't make any sense. Distal clavicle excision. It kept sounding like one of those electronica groups." Henry chuckles and shakes his head.

"What happened? Did you cancel the operation?"

"No. It was fine. Once I got in there, I was fine. I mean, I still couldn't name all the parts I was working on, but it didn't seem to matter. The procedure went fine. He's alive, he'll have full clavicular rotation in no time."

My heart starts thumping again in the panicky way it's been doing lately. "Maybe you should take some time off?"

"No. I'm fine," Henry says, suddenly impatient. "I was just saying, it was funny, that's never happened to me before." I study him, his profile, his smile. I want to touch his face, feel the gray-specked stubble there. He's new. I don't even know him. "But I think it happens all the time," he continues to say, "to doctors at different points in their careers. I mean, I went through something traumatic. I died and came back to life."

"I saved you."

"You saved me."

"How's your head?" I ask, and now it's OK to reach out and touch him, the mark on his forehead. The stitches are out and most of the redness is gone, just a faint shape. Jeremy was right, it did look vaguely like an eighteen on its side, though I think it looks more like a sideways figure eight.

"Infinity underlined," I say.

"It's fine. Not even sore anymore."

I put my hand down. "Are you still hearing things?"

"If by things you mean music, yes, it wakes me up, it's all I can hear."

"Maybe you should see someone."

He doesn't say anything and we drive in silence for a few blocks. I look out at the houses lining the street, generous sturdy constructions in shades of rain, some of which I occasionally entered for dinner parties, some a part of my childhood, where I furtively got drunk, lost control, lost my virginity, lost time. I make a mental note to call Roy and tell him about the music in Henry's head.

At the stop sign, Henry pauses and runs the wiper blades over the ash that had begun to collect on the windshield. He turns to me. "Are you jealous?"

"What?"

"I've finally found something I'm really passionate about, I mean, I really believe I've been given this gift, and you act like I'm sick or something. Jeremy has found his thing, something that has nothing to do with you that makes him happy, and that upsets you, doesn't it?" He slowly shakes his head. "It's like all you've ever done is ask us to leave you alone, and now that we have, you can't stand it."

His face is red, his burgeoning scar glows against his flesh like a button, and when did he get this angry? "I never asked you to leave me alone," I manage to say, reaching out and pressing gently on the scar. I lean over and put my mouth on his. It's soft and wet and longing rushes through me.

Someone honks behind us and Henry turns his face. I wonder if he felt what I felt. Can that much desire be one-sided?

As we pull into the parking lot, I notice a dark funnel of smoke winding into the shadowy sky. "Look," I say, trying to break the tension. I nod to it, a twisted arm pointing in our general direction. "The apocalypse." We get out of the car, doors slamming shut in sync.

"Bring on the three-headed beast," Henry says, and I'm relieved he isn't angry anymore, or is at least pretending not to be. I link my arm through his and we walk into the school.

※

"Sorry for having you come out with these fires, this smoke," Mrs. Sams says, waving her hands around the room as if the whole place is on fire. "I hope it's not near your home?"

"Not yet," I replied, "Thank God."

Mrs. Sams frowns. "Are you religious, Mrs. Barker?"

I glance at Henry and he's grinning. "No, not particularly."

Mrs. Sams then turns to him. "Jeremy, was he raised with religious ideas, the Bible, youth group, that kind of thing?"

Henry shakes his head. "No. He's a boy with his own ideas, his own spirituality, seeming not to be influenced by us in the slightest," he says. "Thank God," he repeats, chuckling. I put my hand on Henry's leg. He doesn't move it.

Mrs. Sams frowns again, the outline of her lips puckering like dried paint. "I've noticed some very elaborate drawings on some of Jeremy's homework, Jesus on the cross, angels, apocalyptic images." Mrs. Sams opens the file folder in front of her and pulls a piece of paper out. "Like this one, for example." She slides it across the desk and I hold it up so we can both see. At the bottom of a series of long-division equations, there's a full-color depiction of a beast, some kind of lion-tiger-wolf, teeth bared, flames roiling out of its mouth, rearing up on hind legs. It's breathtaking. As a piece of art, I can't help but admire it—color like a garish tattoo, just enough childish slant to make it interesting. It's the sort of thing that's really in at the moment, a return to fairy-tale horror combined with off-hue minimalism. And the exploration of religious iconography: it shows a constructive, playful dissection of institution.

"Well?" Mrs. Sams asks. "What do you think?"

I shake my head. "I don't know. It's very interesting."

"So he draws on his homework. I don't know that I see the problem, Mrs. Sams," Henry says, fingering the mark on his forehead.

"Well, Mr. Barker, the problem is that it's gone further than that." Mrs. Sams opens the folder again and this time takes out a Ziploc plastic bag. "I found this on him yesterday." She holds the plastic bag between two fingers and sets it in front of us.

Henry opens it and coughs. "Jesus, that's awful," he says, trying to reseal the bag as quickly as possible. "What the hell is that?"

"It's some kind of animal paw. It seems to have been separated from the animal for quite some time, as you can tell by the smell, Mr. Barker."

Something is vibrating up my throat. I wonder if I should just come clean, tell Henry that I knew about this, that I tried to stop it. But how did Jeremy even get the paw back? Was it a different paw? For all I knew, he'd been collecting them—there've been a lot of coyote attacks in the neighborhood. Who was keeping track of all those paws?

"I'd been noticing that smell for a while now," Mrs. Sams says, "but I couldn't figure out what it was. Then yesterday, during a spelling test, I happened to notice Jeremy rubbing that thing against his ear. I waited until the end of the day, requesting that he stay after class. When I asked for it, he handed it right over. But he said that God talked to him through it, and that he would need it back." Mrs. Sams leans back and looks at us intently. I hate her smugness. She probably doesn't have any kids of her own. It's easy to judge from the outside. "So, Mr. and Mrs. Barker, I was wondering if this incident is symptomatic of a larger situation. Sanitation concerns aside, I think you'll agree this is very disturbing behavior."

I stand up, the room suddenly unbearably small. "We'll take care of it. Thank you, Mrs. Sams, for bringing this to our attention."

Henry shrugs and shakes Mrs. Sams' hand. "It was nice to finally meet you, we'll be in touch," he says, and follows me out.

"Are you in a hurry to get somewhere?" he asks as we get back into the car.

"That woman was a bitch."

"I think she's just concerned."

"Well, I think she could have handled it differently."

"I'm guessing she was a little freaked out."

"Why do you have that thing?"

Henry looks down at the Ziploc bag in his lap. "I didn't even notice."

I've been trying to make Henry jealous all night, but he doesn't seem to be paying any attention. Now Roy is drunk and keeps whispering in my ear, thinking my flirtation is legitimate.

"I've always liked you," he says now, much too close to my face, his breath sour, full of garlic and wine. He's trapped me in the kitchen, blocking the door with his short, thick-chested frame.

"That's sweet, Roy, I should be getting back out there," I say, trying to step back and around him.

"I don't think so," he says, snakes his arm around my back, "Henry doesn't need you quite yet. I think we should get to know each other a little more."

A different time, I probably would have let him snake his arm further, kiss my neck. The cheap thrill of doing something like that with Henry and Jeremy in the other room. But the thought of it now makes me sick. I'm beginning to feel the smoke, like a drug or something falling on top of me, compressing my insides and at the same time making me feel swollen. My neck grows hot and my mouth fills with saliva. I cough, my eyes sting and well.

"This smoke," I say and wave my hand in front of my face.

"What's going on in here?" Henry asks, suddenly in the doorway of the kitchen, glass of wine in his hand, gripping the stem like a hammer.

Roy moves back, grabs a bottle of wine from the counter in one smooth motion. "Just getting some more wine. Penny's out, and you know how she can get if she starts to sober up, like a baby without its tit. Excuse me," he says, squeezing between both of us.

"Tell me you're not having an affair with that guy."

"I'm not having an affair."

"Not right now."

"Never. I only want you." I reach out to put my hand around the back of his neck but he steps back.

"Just don't."

I let my hand fall to my side.

"I'm going to play my piece in five minutes," he says, then turns around and walks out.

I force myself to take a couple deep breaths, swallowing back the burning in my throat. I can't leave the kitchen. None of the people in the next room are my friends. They're all people Henry knows from work, a couple neighbors I don't have anything in common with. I wonder what Henry knows about my past indiscretions. I've always just assumed he knew nothing, and that was why it worked.

"Learn a lesson from the fig tree. When its branch becomes tender and sprouts leaves, you know that summer is near. In the same way, when you see all these things, know that he is near, at the gates," Jeremy says, looking up at me. Where did he come from, how long had he been standing there? He never walks into a room anymore. He appears. He materializes. He is creeping me out.

"Jeremy, where did you come from?"

"It's almost time, Mom."

"OK, honey, I'll be in there in a minute."

He looks at me with a peculiar expression, wrinkling his forehead and smiling. That's when I notice he's holding something at his side.

"Show me what's in your hand," I say, suddenly alarmed. He holds out the cat's paw and I grab it from him. It's still surprisingly soft. "Where did you get this?" I ask him.

"God told me where it was. In the drawer."

"Go listen to your father play."

Jeremy shrugs and leaves. I want to call him to me, put my arms around him, squeeze until the funny feeling in my chest goes away, squeeze the creepy out of him.

Instead, I lean against the counter as piano notes drift in. It's beautiful, a simple, bright melody that conjures kites soaring through a periwinkle sky, warm soft sand, clean white sidewalks. I think about the time right after Henry and I were married, when I was four months pregnant with

Jeremy—after the morning sickness ended, before I became a beach ball, when I was solid and blooming with life. We spent the day at the Santa Monica Pier acting like kids. Henry stuffed himself with cotton candy and corn dogs, and I still thought that was cute. We rode the carousel, making goofy faces at each other in the lit mirrors. On the Ferris wheel, we kissed until we reached the top and then everything—every glittering, sea-glanced thing—was ours.

I realize the music has stopped. In fact, there isn't any sound. Walking into the living room, I hold my breath: no one. It's as if I'd wished them out of existence. Relieved, I take a deep breath, the smoke hardly anything. Nothing but soothing silence. I sit down at the piano bench, picking up the glass of wine that was probably Henry's, pristine but for the greasy stem, still full.

And just as suddenly, I feel uneasy. The room seems to swell, hot with absent bodies. "Hello?" I call out. Nothing.

I get up and inspect the other rooms. I run upstairs, look in all the bedrooms. "Anybody here?" My voice goes out and comes right back, ricocheting off all the tight, impeccably placed surfaces.

I pick up the ukulele lying on our bed and pluck a string. The metallic note reverberates in my chest until it becomes a thin line of pitch I feel faintly in my shoulder blades.

And then I hear something else. Human sounds, muffled laughter.

I go to the window and there they all are on the front lawn. Henry has his guitar and Jeremy's kicking up leaves, and people are laughing and dancing. There is moonlight. The smoke has finally broken.

How silly, what did I think, that the world had ended?

I unlatch the window, to call out to them, let them know I'm coming, that I'll be right down. Silver light casts a feeling of good cheer over the scene, like everyone is alive and glad about that. My fingers remain on the latch. I don't open the window.

I realize I'm still holding the cat paw. It's soft and comforting between my fingers, like the rabbit's foot I used to keep as a girl for good luck. I turn it around bone-end up and inspect it. It really isn't so bad, the gore has mostly dried. And the smell, while definitely strong, is reassuring, familiar. I bring it closer to my mouth.

"Hello?" I call into it. "Hello? Is there anyone there?"

BESTIARY VII: Laundromat Bobcat

This bobcat looks much like the one found in the glossy pages of your *National Geographic*: long legs, large paws, tufted ears similar to those of their larger relative the lynx. Most are brown or brownish red with a white underbelly and short, black-tipped tail, which appears to be cut, or "bobbed." They are fierce hunters and can kill prey twice their size. A solitary animal. They prefer the barnyard cat's hard-boiled autonomy to the codependence of some of the larger wild breeds.

This particular variety of bobcat can be discerned by the sloping back and drooping belly resultant of a life accustomed to lazy dryer afternoons, a glut of unhurried heat-seeking mice. The first one appeared around the time of the contentious mayoral campaign. Some believe our current mayor ultimately won the race due to the hard line she took on preservation. Her opponent was advocating capture and release, and she reacted to this position with considerable public outrage. Her campaign immediately switched gears, from a platform of family values and more park and pool security, to animal-human coexistence. You probably remember those commercials: bobcat stretched out atop the dryer, looking as if it just swallowed a bottle of Vicodin, and our mayor, surrounded by her five angelic children: "For whatever reason, this magnificent beast has chosen our Laundromat as a place it would like to inhabit. Who are we to deny it? Who are we to say, no, bobcat, I'm sorry, but you're sitting on my whites?" The camera panning from her dazzling smile to the coached cherubic faces of her children, then back to the bobcat, which made it appear, at least to the discerning viewer, that they were not even in the same Laundromat. Then the slogan, so catchy you can still hear it recited mockingly on the playground or in the Applebee's parking lot: "Respect the Laundromat Bobcat. Avoid eye contact."

There have been other cats since spotted in and around the Laundromat, and if you can believe the photographs, they have become progressively larger and more ferocious-looking, dagger incisors that no longer fit inside mouths set in bemused satiety. Last month the local paper published the image of a ten-foot trailer unable to fully conceal a set of hulking paws.

There have been disappearances. A dozen or so cats, a few small dogs. A toddler snatched from his backyard, a ten-year-old in the parking lot after swim practice, a female jogger at rosy dusk. It's been rumored that Mrs. Harding, retired divorcée, and Roger Powers, bad-boy bag-boy, were ripped limb from limb one night five years ago, after sneaking into the Laundromat after hours. You usually hear the story from a friend-of-a-friend: scattered organs on the confetti linoleum, sprays of blood across tacked-up ads for t'ai chi in the park, Spanish lessons, missing poodles. But every community must make sacrifices. It's important to maintain some wildness at the edges, to remind people there are boundaries that shouldn't be crossed, natures that just shouldn't be troubled.

Come Closer

It started with Joad's blisters, small red bumps along his knuckles that bloomed into almost beautiful fluid-filled sacs. At first they thought it was the new dish soap, generic stuff Clara bought from the Kroger that was a radioactive green and smelled like apple Jolly Ranchers. But the blisters progressed, even after they threw out the soap and she wrapped each of his fingers in gauze, winding the cotton around palm and wrist. The blisters popped and peeled. Ointment from the doctor didn't do anything except make Joad's hands greasy—then their doorknobs, faucet handles, the fur at the base of their cat's ears.

Then one night, after she'd changed his bandages and they'd climbed into bed, the glowing began. Joad was staring up at the ceiling with his earbuds in, listening to a podcast. Beside him, Clara turned the page of the book she was reading, and it was as if someone held a flashlight under it.

"What?" Joad removed an earbud and squinted at her.

"My book is glowing."

He leaned over and put one of his mummy fingers on the page. "No it's not."

"Yes it is." Clara turned the next page and the glow was even brighter. Black letters swallowed by a pulsing white.

She tried to remember what you were supposed to do. Stop, drop, and roll? Burn the book?

"I feel like you're not taking this seriously," she said.

"It's just the light," Joad said. "The wiring in these old buildings." He reached over her to screw the base of the lamp in tighter, but his bandages prevented him from being effectual.

It was part of Joad's job to be a skeptic. He currently worked as a ghostwriter for a company that helped people communicate with and, if the desire was there, exorcise their ghosts. Telling the story of the dead, the story of the relationship between haunted and hauntee, telling it right, the company claimed, was the only real way to connect— to have control. Hence it was important to root out truth from fantasy, reality from superstition. The ghostwriter had to question everything. Only then could he spin something beautiful, a story that transcended the corporeal. Regular human speech, the prevailing logic went, wasn't good enough—you couldn't just *talk* to your ghost, the dead no longer had ears, or at least not human ones, made for human sound. But a good story could get at the truth, could enter the dreamspace shared with the ghosts and settle the matters that needed to be settled. In this way, the ghostwriters were both medium and artist. They were attuned. It took a certain sensitivity and openness. Joad, it turned out, was special. What used to be liability in his professional life—a cynical nature, an avoidance of reality—had become assets.

"I think it's happening," Clara said.

Neither of them had experienced a haunting before. Both had likely candidates—Joad's favorite aunt, passed away years ago from liver failure; Clara's first boyfriend, car crash senior year of high school; his college roommate; Clara's grandmother.

There were moments. The lights would flicker, the cat rigid as a statue. Clara would wake in the middle of the night to her heart beating wildly for no discernible reason. But nothing ever materialized, and they'd assumed their dead ones were content.

The glow evolved. At school the next day, Clara sat down for design theory and the chalkboard gleamed palely. In perfect neat script there was written in the corner *I too am not a bit tamed, I too am untranslatable.* Goosebumps on the back of her neck. She'd forgotten about V. The room suddenly warm, scent of vanilla and crushed leaves. When V was alive, she would recite these lines every time she saw a hawk, or when someone on the subway asked where she was from.

Dr. Wheeler began to talk about color, his voice low and disinterested, and Clara saw the blue in V's hair, how it would change depending on the light, from sky to stone to Windex. Clara would casually drop by her apartment those nights Joad worked late. Billie Holiday on the record player. Something delicious bubbling on the stove. In candlelight: the ocean at dusk.

"Black is the strongest of the neutral colors," Dr. Wheeler was saying. He clicked through slides of websites with severe black borders.

Clara saw the warm brown of her skin, the pink beds of her nails, the dark bark of scab on her knee, pollen flecks in her eyes.

Clara had always been good at compartmentalizing, putting things in discreet boxes and looking at them only when absolutely necessary. But these images hovered just beyond her control like a vivid dream, one that upon waking can neither be chased nor banished.

Dr. Wheeler moved to the chalkboard, raised his hand and erased the poem. Chalk dust, more than seemed possible, hovered, causing him to cough and wave his hand around in front of his watering eyes.

Shortly after the first reports, Clara had decided to go back to school—something about the confirmation of an afterlife had made her realize the importance of an education—and, since she got into the University of Cincinnati's design school with a scholarship, and Joad worked from home anyway, they'd moved to Cincinnati, a city that, it seemed to Clara, could use a good architect, or a more benevolent god. The streets on a loop instead of a grid, forever leading you back to where you started, the freeways under constant construction, perpetual pounding and smoke, whole parts of the city coned off. People who called you *Honey* and *Sugar* but didn't look you in the eye.

After class, Dr. Wheeler asked to speak with her. She stood beside the podium as the other students shuffled out. One of them, a girl with whom Clara had formed a kind of note-sharing alliance, made the sign of the cross. Dr. Wheeler was notorious for his meanness, his lack of empathy in dealing with students. In his sixties, with a full head of white hair and pale blue eyes that bore right into yours through to the gray gelatinous matter that, he hated to point out, was unforgivably lacking. Clara braced herself.

"Your last paper," he began.

She swallowed. It had not been her best work. She'd written about font, a diatribe entitled *Ten Reasons to Hate Comic Sans*. Number one: It was created for a cartoon dog.

"Though not particularly academic, or new," he continued, "it displays a keen insight, good judgment."

"Thank you," she said.

He looked to the wall behind her, his brow wrinkled, as if there was something on a teleprompter he didn't want to say.

"I was hoping you'd help me with something," he finally said. Clara waited for him to continue, though after a minute, it was unclear whether or not he would.

"What is it?"

"I heard you know a ghostwriter," he said. "Your boyfriend?"

Where would he have heard this? She didn't think she'd told anyone what Joad did for a living.

"Yes," she said hesitantly.

"I don't want to put you in an awkward position," he said. "But the wait list is so long, and I was hoping—I'll pay, of course."

"You want him to write a story for you?"

Dr. Wheeler's face reddened and he looked away.

"I'll ask him," she said quickly, to save them both further discomfort, though she was doubtful. Joad was protective of his work, and he liked to follow the rules. "I can't promise anything."

"Oh, thank you," he said. He put a hand to his heart and sighed, a gesture that seemed uncharacteristic, much more graceful than his classroom gruff, and Clara wondered what his private life was like, what secrets he might keep.

⁘

Nothing else happened for the rest of the afternoon. When Clara got home, Joad was sitting at the kitchen table in front of his computer, elbows on the table, hands up in a position of surrender.

"What's for dinner?" she asked, setting her books on the counter. On the floor at her feet the cat's dish was covered in ants again. No matter how many they killed, more came up through the floorboards.

"Whatever you want," he said. "Chicken?"

She grabbed the cat dish from the floor and set it in the sink.

"How was school?" he asked.

"Fine. Kind of strange," she said. "My professor asked me to stay after class."

"Did you get in trouble?" He was half-listening, clicking through something on his computer. "Hey, check this out." He turned the screen to show her a picture of a woman: big sunglasses, hair like a soft brown cloud. Stenciled in sunlight, mid-stride down a street, navy blue button-down shirt, a single strand of pearls.

"Who is it?"

"You don't recognize her?"

Clara shook her head. Joad usually didn't talk about his customers. It was against company policy; they had a strict confidentiality agreement, the nature of disclosed information being very private and highly volatile—any kind of manipulation by the outside world could change everything. But sometimes he couldn't help himself.

"Jacqueline Kennedy Onassis."

She looked closer. "That doesn't even look like her."

"Did you know she was an editor for Doubleday?"

"Your customer is being haunted by Jackie O?" She took the chicken out of the refrigerator. It had the same glow as her novel the night before: a cool white throb. Haunted book, haunted chicken. *Okay*, she thought, *let's do this*. The glow intensified as she cut away the plastic.

"He claims to have dated her granddaughter right before her death."

Most of Joad's clients were found not to have a ghost. It was important for the integrity of the company to first establish the veracity of the haunting claim, so success rates could also be verified, though either way, the story got written.

"You don't think it's her?" Clara peeled garlic while keeping an eye on the chicken.

"Very flimsy evidence so far." He clicked through some more images. "A feeling. Some French whispered in the early morning hours."

"French?"

"She was fluent."

Clara took out the little pouch of organs from the cavity of the chicken. Pushed the raw cloves of garlic underneath the skin. The light drew in and around the knobs of leg bone she tied with twine.

Joad got up and stood behind her. She leaned back and he put his arms around her, both of them holding their hands out, the affection of untouchables.

He brushed the top of her head with his lips. "Do you still think you're being haunted?"

She nodded against his chin.

"Who do you think it is?"

This seemed very much a question he was avoiding, mishearing and actively resisting. For this reason, she told him. Joad just cocked his head and then shook it vaguely.

"Who?"

"You remember her. Our neighbor from that studio in Portland."

"The girl with the accent? She played the clarinet?"

"Trombone."

"She was wild, always locking herself out, always out of breath. And that hair."

"Yeah."

"Yeah yeah, now I remember—cancer, right? Breast?" He moved to the refrigerator and took out some lettuce and a cucumber. "Why do you think it's her?" He began to chop on the cutting board beside her.

She looked at him until he stopped chopping. She wanted him to see. She needed him to look into her and understand. Those months she'd been with V, when every cell of her body flickered alive and everything else—the leaves on the trees, the scudding clouds in the blue sky, the worm writhing on the sidewalk—was also more alive. He didn't know, he couldn't see it.

"What? What is it? You want me to write a story?" He smiled, like he knew what she wanted and that he was the only one who could give it to her, but would only give it to her if she acknowledged her need.

She returned to the chicken. "My professor asked me to ask you for one."

"A story?"

"I don't even know how he knew."

"Word gets around." He loved this, being known for something, having something other people wanted.

Joad began to make the dressing and soon they fell into their old synchronicity, moving together and apart like magnets. Once the chicken went into the oven, it stopped glowing. Nothing else happened for the rest of the night, though Clara still felt her presence. It hovered over them while they ate then watched bad TV then went to bed, while Joad put his mouth on her neck and she backed into him and touched herself and moaned in the dark.

Shouting in a hallway. They'd just moved in and hadn't met any of their neighbors yet. Clara was carrying groceries and out of breath from the stairs and wondered if she should call the police.

A shockingly beautiful girl was yelling that it was the middle of the day, that she could play her music as loud as she wanted, that this *cunt*, or Mrs. O'Keefe, as Clara would come to know her, was a shut-in bore who could use a little music in her life, and Mrs. O'Keefe was shouting back through her cracked front door that she was going to call immigration, have the girl shipped back to whatever mosquito-infested third-world country she came from.

Clara put her bag of groceries down and fumbled for her keys. V leaned against Mrs. O'Keefe's doorframe. She wore light yellow pajama pants with ice cream cones on them. Looked up at her. Glared, on fire with something Clara didn't have a name for yet.

The next time Clara saw her was at a bar. V was there in a red silk shirt playing trombone on a makeshift stage. Nobody was listening. She sang in Portuguese in the space between the notes. She didn't look at the audience. She looked down and sang softly. A thick black snake writhed and coiled around her neck, down her arms. This might have been a dream.

In the produce aisle. A girl suddenly so close Clara could feel the heat from her arm as she pointed out a bird that swooped underneath the fluorescents. The kind of girl Clara had always admired from a distance: tough and smudged and sure. The two of them dropping Granny Smiths into plastic bags. A second-hand prom dress, black and dramatic, showed off her tattoos, the wood table with legs that tapered from her shoulder blades, twisted into tree roots at the small of her back.

The images had begun to coalesce, to gather power and shape. This remembering and imagining was a conscious act, a step onto a ledge. When Clara did it, she felt V grow stronger. She knew she should stop, it was making Joad sick. The blisters had gotten worse. They'd spread, frothing up his wrists.

In addition to the blisters now, he'd begun to glow.

Almost imperceptible at first, now a warm peach gleam that seemed part of his skin. It looked almost healthy, like he was in love.

He continued to work, sometimes late into the night. Client volume was increasing every day, and the blisters kept him from sleep. Sometimes when Clara would get up to check on him, he'd be at the kitchen table hunched over his computer, glowing brighter than his screen. He didn't notice it, didn't let on that anything was wrong—but it couldn't be good for him. He went back to the doctor for the blisters, but she said it was a simple irritation: there must be something he was using, a soap or lotion that he should stop using.

Name: James R. Wheeler

Date: 4/30/18

Occupation: Professor of Design, University of Cincinnati

Sex: M

Age: 47

Ghost's name: Valerie Alvarado

Details of death: Metastatic breast cancer

Nature of relationship (please be as specific as possible):
Romantic; met a year before she was diagnosed. From the beginning, it felt as if she had stolen a vital organ, as if someone had discovered something new about the universe that changed everything. I wasn't strong enough. I didn't know how to handle it, all that feeling. I couldn't risk it. I tried for a while, pretended to have the courage, to be the kind of person who sees something beautiful and thinks: I deserve to be in the company of this beauty. I couldn't stop thinking of things to do for her. Would leave flowers or love poems or empanadas from her favorite

Peruvian joint or pages ripped from my favorite novels in front of her door. Would wait there with them, hoping she would sense my presence and open the door. When we talked, it felt like the release of a great pressure, time would thicken, slow, as if moving through honey, and when we didn't talk, it felt equally amazing, like maybe we would never speak again, like we would live like mollusks under the sea, passing sand back and forth between our lips. When we kissed (is there a way to say this, any of it, without sounding so corny? Is this even relevant?), it was hard to breathe. It was hard to know what body parts belonged to which person, and it was hard to remember simple things like to eat food and that I had to go to work at particular times and that I lived with someone else and needed to go home. When she got sick, I thought I would leave, I would dedicate myself to her, to nursing her. The last time I saw her, she let me touch her stitches. A row of tiny wire teepees an inch below her nipple. I rubbed my cheek against them like a cat. It wasn't serious, she said. They were being careful. A routine procedure. It happened so quickly, it turned so fast. I thought there would be more time.

Any unfinished business, grudges, promises unkept, or other relevant details:
YES.

One of their parties. V had come by herself. They invited all the neighbors whenever they had a party, folded a written invitation into each mailbox, to engender goodwill and leniency when the noise continued late into the night, which included their phone number to be used, hopefully, in lieu of law enforcement.

That point in the night when the fuzziness had grown over, the shade that lurked at the edges, people who hours

earlier had been charming and gracious, the most inter-
esting people she knew, now arrogant pricks, each trying
to out-anecdote the others. V was sitting by herself on the
floor, back against the wall. She so inhabited her body that
she seemed to transcend it. Utterly uninterested in the peo-
ple around her, but not bored either—as if simply existing
was enough.

Though they'd run into each other a handful of times,
they hadn't yet done this, made a concerted effort to be in
the same room. Clara was curious about her in that way she
sometimes got about women, a feeling like she wanted to be
trapped in a dark space with her and also like she wanted
to borrow her clothes, draw her nails along the frail bones
of her wrist.

"I like your tattoos," Clara said. In addition to the
wood table across V's shoulder blades that morphed into a
tree across her back there was darkly inked music on the
undersides of both her arms, tabs with sprays of notes, an
intricate notation like barbed wire. Clara was afraid to ask
her what they were, probably part of some famous piece of
classical music she should recognize.

"Do you have any?" V asked.

Clara squatted next to her on the floor. "One."

"A butterfly on your ankle." Plosives like delicate stones
in her mouth. V reached out and touched her ankle, just
a quick flick of her finger, but it took Clara's legs out from
under her.

"Close."

"Dolphin at the small of your back." She lifted the back
of her shirt and Clara turned so she could look. V traced the
top lace of Clara's underwear above the waist of her jeans.

"Closer." Clara's heart was beating too fast and she be-
gan to tremble.

"Hummingbird above hip bone," V said, her lips at Clara's ear. "Is this close enough?"

⁘

Joad and Clara decided to go out. The restaurant put white linen over the tables and charged fine-dining prices, even though the food was better suited to a truck or stand. But it felt like a real date. Candles, a bottle of wine. Joad glowed across from her like a nightlight, and she tried to sneak looks at the other diners to see if they could see it too, but if they did, they pretended not to.

"It feels nice to be out of the house," he said. He looked around and smiled, like it wasn't just a bunch of white people eating Caesar salad.

"Yeah. Sorry. I feel like I haven't been home much."

"You're busy." Joad set his elbows on the table, then crossed his arms, then put his hands in his lap. No matter what he did, he didn't seem able to get comfortable. "I'm just glad you suggested this." His fingers were swollen to almost twice their size, each wrapped in gauze. He wore a long-sleeved button-up shirt, but she could tell the cuffs bothered his wrists. She felt a familiar tug of sympathy and warmth. She loved him. She had always loved him.

"How's work?" she asked, ripping into a breadstick. "How's Dr. Wheeler's case going?"

"Case. I like that. It's coming along. I have a first draft."

"Already?" She'd given him the form the day before, in an envelope with two one-hundred-dollar bills, standard ghostwriter retainer. She changed only logistical details— it was the big picture that was important, she reasoned, the larger thematic thrust of the haunting.

"I think so," he said. "I mean, I think it's pretty good. My best yet. I took some liberties." He grinned.

"But aren't you supposed to stick to the facts, more or less?"

"To be honest, there are some inconsistencies." He finished the rest of his glass of wine and wince-poured another. He was drinking more than usual. "I don't think your professor is telling the whole truth."

There was a sudden commotion at the back of the restaurant. A woman making loud noises, what sounded like wolf howls. Her companion looked embarrassed, shrugging at the rest of them, like, *What am I supposed to do we all know the drill by now it could be madness or haunting I don't bother asking the question anymore.*

"Yeah, but you're supposed to stick as close to the truth as possible, right, or it won't work. You can't just take his money. You're deceiving him."

"Don't worry," he said. He shook his glowing locks. He reached his hand across the table, and they both stared at the bandages. "He'll never know. These things, these stories, they really don't work anyway. Why are you getting so mad?"

"What do you mean they don't work?"

The waiter came and put their food down, but she couldn't eat. She watched as Joad shoveled food into his mouth, his bandaged hands like big clunky paws.

"I don't know, not for sure. I mean, how can anyone? If we don't know the rules, we can't exactly follow them. A ghost could go away and come back the next week, or the next year. Or another one could show up. Or the ghost could be a figment of the imagination."

"Glad to hear you've finally found a job you can believe in."

He put down his fork, set his bandaged hands on either side of his plate.

"I don't know what's going on with you," he said. "But something definitely is."

-:::-

There was the time they went to the coast for the weekend. It was near the end. Not the end-end, but the last time they were really together. Before her diagnosis. Clara told Joad she was meeting an old friend from high school. He didn't even ask her any follow-up questions, never mind that it was a name she made up on the spot.

It was winter so they got a good deal on a nice hotel right on the water. Too cold to go outside so they stayed inside while the wind shook the windows and the ocean crashed and crashed. They barely slept or ate. Clara learned things about her own body she hadn't known before, places on it that, pressed or scratched or licked, would make her tremble and cry out.

The early morning hours were her favorite, when neither of them was fully awake or asleep, their physical bodies spent, the sky just beginning to lighten, V's lips at her ear half-murmuring stories, the tickle of her breath, the softness of her breasts pressed against her back. Those were the moments it seemed like they had all the time in the world, that time would wait for them, that it would allow them to stretch it into a long country highway they could walk forever.

On their last night, V decided to take a bath. Clara suggested she join her, but V declined. She needed to get clean, she said, before she got very very dirty.

As soon as V closed the bathroom door behind her, Clara went rigid with fear. Literally. She couldn't move her body. She lay on top of the bed's slippery coverlet, her hands in fists beside her. Nothing like this had ever happened to her before. It was as if the connection between mind and body had been severed. As she lay there listening to the water run then shut off, the sounds of V moving, shifting, in the bath, humming something Clara couldn't place, she had the unshakable feeling that something terrible was happening. Something unnameable. A darkness that crept in from the outside, that had slithered its way through the cracks of the window, had come in with them and waited, feeding on the dust of other people's skin trapped under the bed, growing bigger with all that hate and sex and salt. It had waited until one of them was alone.

She tried counting her breaths in and out. She tried concentrating on the blank stucco of the ceiling. But there was that door, the sound of the bathroom door closing, the sound of the lock clicking into place.

Just when Clara thought she couldn't take any more, that she would literally break in two, V emerged from the bathroom trailing steam, a fluffy white towel wrapped around her body, one wrapped around her hair like a turban. Her skin glistened and the smell of hotel soap filled the room.

"Are you okay?" she asked, seeing Clara lying there like that. "What's wrong?"

"I don't know," she managed to say, her body returning, shivering. "Come closer."

⁙

A new report said the best thing you can do is forget. Though each haunting was an individual experience, they'd discovered a common progression. It began with little things: a flicker of shadow, music, a line written on a piece of paper. Then a glow. A light that gathered in unlikely places, that took hold of an object or person and colonized. As the glowing progressed, researchers said, memories of the one who passed, of the haunter, gathered momentum and mass. If the haunted was able to keep these memories and sensations to a minimum, they said, the glowing usually ceased, or became manageably dim. If left unchecked, if indulged, the results were harder to predict, but it seemed to not be good. Sickness, injury, sometimes death of the glowing.

This was not a good thing, career-wise, for Joad. If people believed that ignoring the haunting was the best course of action, the entire business model upon which his job rested would be called into question. He'd become more sullen and irritable than usual. All he did was work; whenever she came home from class, walked into the kitchen, he would be furiously typing away, wouldn't even look up. He no longer shared with her the details of what he was working on. When she asked, he would act put-upon. Affronted.

"You know I can't share that information with you. Why would you even ask?"

On the news, reports of inflictions increased. Mostly celebrities and politicians. The son of the singer of a famous rock band whose song was in everyone's head, played on every station and piped into every store, so weak he had to be hospitalized. The Vice President's wife, a sustained fever, an induced coma. His words played over images of bodies wheeled on carts, wrapped in sheets.

"Please, be careful with your prayers."

A noise woke Clara. She wasn't sure what it was, but the longer she lay there, the surer she was that it was something. A faint hiss followed by a click. Like the needle on a record between tracks, an oxygen machine, the pneumatic wheeze of bus doors, a ghost adding up all her sins. She looked over at Joad, a nimbus of peach light around his curled form. She thought about waking him, but it seemed impossible, and possibly dangerous, to reach over and touch him. Quietly she got out of bed and tried to follow the sound, but it fizzled in the hallway to a low buzz.

Light flickered from Joad's laptop open on the kitchen counter. She came closer. A tickle at the back of her neck. Her mind flashed to the night she and V went to the roller derby with a flask of whiskey, then got on skateboards and rolled down the steepest hill in the city, laughing and bloody all the way home. The slow fucking and crying. Her sickness. The lump Clara had found, the look they exchanged in that moment, like they both knew what was going to happen, could see into the terrible future, both wanting to stop time, to turn it back, to play it again. Joad's laptop glowed brighter. A sound oozed up from the linoleum, a muffled musical moan. Clara held her breath in order to hear it better. It stopped. She moved toward the glowing screen carefully, crumbs sticking to the bottoms of her feet, her breath ragged and shallow, dread gathering at the nape of her neck.

She sat down in front of the computer and began to read. *It started with Joad's blisters, small red bumps along his knuckles that bloomed into almost beautiful fluid-filled sacs. At first they thought it was the new dish soap, generic stuff Clara got from the Kroger that was a radioactive green and smelled like apple Jolly Ranchers.* She heard someone behind her. Bandaged hands on her shoulders. Breath in her ear.

"Is this close enough?"

BESTIARY VIII: The Alligators

It had to do with our souls. The number of sick pets and ex-tramarital affairs had increased. It seemed there were more paper-cuts that year. People complained of being unable to look away, unable to act—we watched from our porches the ambulance try to find the correct address, the coyote saun-ter up to the neighbor's kitty, the young girl from down the street get into a stranger's car, the air turn from invis-ible to murky with beetles. Black and winged, they liked to amass around doorways and windows, reminding us of our daily thresholds, those terrible moments of in-between. If you forgot to cover your pool—a dozen or so churning the water, swallowed by children with eyes squeezed shut *Marco*-ing in the presumed safety of their own backyard.

There was finally a meeting called at the town hall. The problem was, nobody could really pin down what the prob-lem was. We could get rid of the beetles, sure, but everyone agreed that barely brushed the surface of the real issue. Mrs. Lancaster suggested a new church—shiny pews, stained-glass windows blinding as the word of God—but most of us felt this solution would benefit only a small segment of the population. A new newspaper, painting classes, t'ai chi in the park—considered and then discarded. We needed something not to distract but inspire, remind us why we go to the trouble.

Alligators were big that year. Stories and videos were making the rounds; something about their prehistoric muck, their capacity for violence, seemed to capture the public imagination.

We ordered them from a catalogue. When they showed up, recently hatched, a dozen in a secure tub, they were so small they could fit in an infant's hand. Speckled as quail eggs, the grim set of their tiny jaws amused, like grumpy old men. We took turns caring for them in our bathtubs and kiddie pools. It was not unusual to walk by a neighbor's house and hear him inside cooing, "Who's a tough guy? You're a tough guy."

By the time we released them into the lake, the beetles had practically disappeared; the ones left remained hidden inside our hedges, high in the branches of our jacarandas.

Some of our other problems seemed to have disappeared, too. We were more conscientious. If someone was crossing the street, we waited until they were safely on the sidewalk before moving the car forward. More eye contact, smiles exchanged, friendly conversation in line at the grocery store. The alligators seemed to have opened us up, exposing our stingy boundaries, the hoarding of our privacy.

If someone was feeling down, we'd say, "Pick up that lizard tail," meaning, "Stop feeling sorry for yourself." Or, if we felt someone was judging us unfairly: "Don't be a hater, Alligator."

We heard all sorts of things from the surrounding towns—we were in a cult practicing black magic, which we intended to unleash on the other towns in a grand apocalyptic gesture. Or we were keeping the alligators for medical experiments, practicing new methods of plastic surgery and organ harvesting. Perhaps my favorite: we were using their skin for our international shoe and handbag export business.

To put the rumors to rest, we decided to throw a Fourth of July party by Alligator Lake and invite some of our friends from the neighboring towns to join us. We bought truckloads of hot dogs and champagne with the rest of the year's available funds, more fireworks than we were legally supposed to have. We hired a local folk trio.

A good turnout: fifty or so people from outside our town, almost everyone from inside. Children ran around with Popsicles and sparklers (a strict no-swimming rule). The alligators remained half-submerged along the lake's shore in the shallow warmer water, grinning like fools. We threw them a couple hot dogs.

"I gotta hand it to you," one of the other-towners said, "you've got something pretty special here." And we agreed: it was inexplicable, the feeling that day. As if our savage natures were no longer submerged in the dark recesses of our subconscious but right there in the open—an external menace that made us better than ourselves, challenged us into grace.

But as the sun went down and we, drunk, heavy with food, cuddled together on blankets, something shifted. Was it the crack of fireworks? The perceived threat of strangers in the dark? Or had the alligators been waiting all along, biding their time for the perfect moment to finally enact the nightmare we had initiated?

The screaming started on the north edge. It's hard to differentiate at this point between what happened and the stories. In our collective imagination, the alligators rose altogether from the muck, one beast made of steel mud and gaping jaws. Our uncles and daughters. Our teachers and veterinarians. The mayor. Most of the people from the other towns. Their spree was not total; they left some of us, those farthest away from the lake, or just not in the direct line of their murder.

Some people, afterward, said it was a cleansing. The alligators only took those who deserved it, who had committed crimes or harbored darkness in their hearts.

But most of us who remain know better. Most of us realize, now, that concepts like *deserved* are no longer applicable.

Stuffed and lacquered, the alligators now sit grinning their terrible grins in front of the town hall, with a plaque: In Loving Memory.

But in loving memory of whom, exactly? Those we'd lost? The alligators? And isn't that the problem, ultimately, too much love in our memories, too much nostalgia in our history? When will we own up to the fact that we ourselves are animals, most fully alive as we stalk and slink and howl—and maybe, the real problem is, that we ever tried to pretend otherwise?

Acknowledgments

I would like to extend my sincere thanks to the editors of the magazines in which stories from this collection, sometimes in slightly different form, first appeared:

The Collagist: "3-D Printing: A Love Story";
Crazyhorse: "The Permutations of A";
Gulf Coast: "Fall from Grace";
Indiana Review: "The Neighbor's Bees" (including "Suburban Fox" and "Attic Raccoon");
The Literary Review: "Dog Story";
The Masters Review: "The First Location";
Matter Journal: "Anatomy Is Destiny";
The Normal School: "Adventures in Wildlife";
The Pinch: "Happy You're Here";
Redivider: "The Rapture Index";
TriQuarterly: "Apocalypso."

Thanks also to all the people who have helped me with these stories over the years and supported me as a writer, with special gratitude to my workshop comrades at the University of Cincinnati and Colorado State University and professors Michael Griffith, Chris Bachelder, Leah Stewart, Steven Schwartz, Leslee Becker, and Judy Doenges. Thank you to the Old Town Writers' Group in Fort Collins. Thank you to Peter Conners and the rest of the BOA team. Thank you to the residencies that allowed me the time and space to write, especially the Millay Colony for the Arts and the Virginia Center for the Creative Arts, where I worked on these stories. Thank you to all the people who inspire and awe me, who are too many to name but I hope you know who you are. Thank you Barbara and Mike Reid, for the love and support. Thank you, Marty: my first reader and best friend.

About the Author

Molly Reid's stories have appeared on NPR and in the journals *Gulf Coast, TriQuarterly, Crazyhorse, Redivider, Indiana Review*, and *The Normal School*, among others. She has received fellowship and residency support from the Bread Loaf Writers' Conference, the Sewanee Writers' Conference, the Millay Colony for the Arts, the Ucross Foundation, I-Park, the Anderson Center, and the Virginia Center for the Creative Arts. Molly is currently a PhD candidate in Fiction at the University of Cincinnati, where she is Associate Editor at *The Cincinnati Review*.

BOA Editions, Ltd. American Reader Series

No. 1 *Christmas at the Four Corners of the Earth*
Prose by Blaise Cendrars
Translated by Bertrand Mathieu

No. 2 *Pig Notes & Dumb Music: Prose on Poetry*
By William Heyen

No. 3 *After-Images: Autobiographical Sketches*
By W. D. Snodgrass

No. 4 *Walking Light: Memoirs and Essays on Poetry*
By Stephen Dunn

No. 5 *To Sound Like Yourself: Essays on Poetry*
By W. D. Snodgrass

No. 6 *You Alone Are Real to Me: Remembering Rainer Maria Rilke*
By Lou Andreas-Salomé

No. 7 *Breaking the Alabaster Jar: Conversations with Li-Young Lee*
Edited by Earl G. Ingersoll

No. 8 *I Carry A Hammer In My Pocket For Occasions Such As These*
By Anthony Tognazzini

No. 9 *Unlucky Lucky Days*
By Daniel Grandbois

No. 10 *Glass Grapes and Other Stories*
By Martha Ronk

No. 11 *Meat Eaters & Plant Eaters*
By Jessica Treat

No. 12 *On the Winding Stair*
By Joanna Howard

No. 13 *Cradle Book*
By Craig Morgan Teicher

No. 14 *In the Time of the Girls*
By Anne Germanacos

No. 15 *This New and Poisonous Air*
By Adam McOmber

Colophon

BOA Editions, Ltd., a not-for-profit publisher of poetry and other literary works, fosters readership and appreciation of contemporary literature. By identifying, cultivating, and publishing both new and established poets and selecting authors of unique literary talent, BOA brings high-quality literature to the public. Support for this effort comes from the sale of its publications, grant funding, and private donations.

The publication of this book is made possible, in part, by the special support of the following individuals:

Anonymous
Angela Bonazinga & Catherine Lewis
James Long Hale
Kelly Hatton & Tom White
Melanie & Ron Martin-Dent
Joe McElveney
Boo Poulin
Deborah Ronnen
Steven O. Russell & Phyllis Rifkin-Russell
Meredith & Adam Smith
William Waddell & Linda Rubel